Unofficial
Harry Styles Crochet

Unofficial Harry Styles Crochet

20+ PROJECTS

Inspired by the Music and Style Icon

Lee Sartori

QUARRY

Quarto.com

© 2025 Quarto Publishing Group USA Inc.
Text © 2025 Lee Sartori

First published in 2025 by Quarry Books, an imprint of The Quarto Group,
100 Cummings Center, Suite 265-D, Beverly, MA 01915, USA.
T (978) 282-9590 F (978) 283-2742

"Helpful Information" (pages 14–15) and "Crochet Techniques" (pages 132–140)
previously published in *The Complete Photo Guide to Crochet*, *2nd Edition*,
by Margaret Hubert © 2014 Creative Publishing international.

All rights reserved. No part of this book may be reproduced in any form without written
permission of the copyright owners. All images in this book have been reproduced
with the knowledge and prior consent of the artists concerned, and no responsibility
is accepted by producer, publisher, or printer for any infringement of copyright or
otherwise, arising from the contents of this publication. Every effort has been made to
ensure that credits accurately comply with information supplied. We apologize for any
inaccuracies that may have occurred and will resolve inaccurate or missing information
in a subsequent reprinting of the book.

Quarry Books titles are also available at discount for retail, wholesale, promotional,
and bulk purchase. For details, contact the Special Sales Manager by email at
specialsales@quarto.com or by mail at The Quarto Group, Attn: Special Sales Manager,
100 Cummings Center, Suite 265-D, Beverly, MA 01915, USA.

10 9 8 7 6 5 4 3 2 1

ISBN: 978-0-7603-9532-5

Digital edition published in 2025
eISBN: 978-0-7603-9533-2

Library of Congress Cataloging-in-Publication Data

Names: Sartori, Lee, author.
Title: Unofficial Harry Styles crochet : 20+ projects inspired by the music
   and style icon / Lee Sartori.
Description: Beverly, MA, USA : Quarry Books, 2025. | Includes index.
Identifiers: LCCN 2024043892 (print) | LCCN 2024043893 (ebook) | ISBN
   9780760395325 (trade paperback) | ISBN 9780760395332 (ebook)
Subjects: LCSH: Crocheting--Patterns. | Styles, Harry, 1994---Influence.
Classification: LCC TT820 .S23655 2025 (print) | LCC TT820 (ebook) | DDC
   746.43/4041--dc23/eng/20241128
LC record available at https://lccn.loc.gov/2024043892
LC ebook record available at https://lccn.loc.gov/2024043893

Crochet project designers: Meghan Ballmer, Jennifer Connors, Julie Desjardins,
Ashlee Elle, Krysten Grymes, Valérie Prieur-Côté, Lee Sartori, Wilma Westenberg
Photography: Nicole Lapierre Photography | lapierrephotography.com
Models: Jill Cochran and Noël Sartori
Illustration: Veronica Carratello
Technical illustration: Kj Hay

Printed in China

To my sons, Noël and Conan. I can't wait to see where your dreams take you.

ACKNOWLEDGMENTS

This is now my sixth published crochet book and still it doesn't lose its magic and sparkle every single time. I couldn't have made this without a few of my friends jumping in to help. Meghan Ballmer, Jennifer Connors, Julie Desjardins, Ashlee Elle, Krysten Grymes, Valérie Prieur-Côté, and Wilma Westenberg, thank you so much! I would also like to thank my husband and best friend, Sean, for always being in my corner, along with my sons, Noël and Conan. And, last but not least, my "too good to be real" editor, Michelle. Thanks for taking me along on another project with you!

Contents

Acknowledgments, 5

Project Gallery, 8

Introduction, 13

Helpful Information, 14

Chapter One: Red Carpet, 16

"Sweet Creature" Sheep Vest, 18

"As It Was" Harry Styles Doll, 24

"Sign of the Times" Black Lace Shawl, 32

"Golden" Cardigan, 38

"Adore You" Strawberry Halter Top, 44

"Watermelon Sugar" Clutch, 50

"Cherry" Earrings, 54

Chapter Two:
Home Sweet Home, 58

"Falling" Patchwork Pullover, 60
Harry's House Pillow, 68
"Music for a Sushi Restaurant" Sushi, 72
"Matilda" Tea and Toast Coasters, 78
"Two Ghosts" Slippers, 84
"Treat People with Kindness" Pillow, 90
"Fine Line" Butterfly Tattoo Blanket, 94

Chapter Three:
Concert Ready, 102

"Satellite" Beanie, 104
Love on Tour Bunnies, 108
"Daylight" Dungaree Blanket, 114
"Sunflower, Vol. 6" Bucket Hat, 118
"Canyon Moon" Market Bag, 122
"Late Night Talking" Scarf, 128

Crochet Techniques, 132

About the Author, 141
Index, 142

Project Gallery

The projects in the book are organized by occasion, and each chapter includes projects for a range of skill levels. The projects are organized here by difficulty level so you can quickly find the projects you want to make first!

Basic

"Music for a Sushi Restaurant" Sushi
Page 72

"Watermelon Sugar" Clutch
Page 50

"Cherry" Earrings
Page 54

"Matilda" Tea and Toast Coasters
Page 78

"Satellite" Beanie
Page 104

EASY

Harry's House Pillow
Page 68

"Sunflower, Vol. 6" Bucket Hat
Page 118

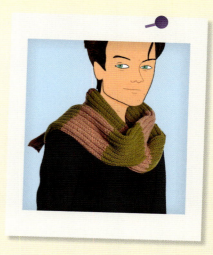

"Late Night Talking" Scarf
Page 128

"As It Was" Harry Styles Doll
Page 24

"Two Ghosts" Slippers
Page 84

Intermediate

Love on Tour Bunnies
Page 108

"Canyon Moon" Market Bag
Page 122

"Treat People with Kindness" Pillow
Page 90

"Daylight" Dungaree Blanket
Page 114

"Fine Line" Butterfly Tattoo Blanket
Page 94

Complex

"Sweet Creature" Sheep Vest
Page 18

"Sign of the Times" Black Lace Shawl Page 32

"Golden" Cardigan
Page 38

"Falling" Patchwork Pullover
Page 60

"Adore You" Strawberry Halter Top
Page 44

Introduction

It's interesting to find out when and where people in my life first heard about Harry Styles. Was it when they saw him perform on *The X Factor*? He was just a young guy back then, working in a bakery and dreaming of making it big. Was it when he joined his bandmates in the famous pop group One Direction? How about when he began acting in films like *Dunkirk* and *Don't Worry Darling*? Or it could have possibly been with the release of any one of his highly acclaimed solo albums in recent years. However you found out about this Grammy-winning artist, one thing is for certain—Harry's star continues to rise higher and higher, and we are here for it!

In this crochet book, we worked to put together some patterns that Harry Styles fans would love and be excited to make. The skill range is pretty broad, with some beginner-friendly patterns and some that are a bit more challenging for those crocheters who have been stitching for a few years. No matter what pattern you choose to start with, I hope you will keep coming back for more and more!

During the making of this book, I was able to share the designs I created along the way with some of my friends and family, and I knew items were a hit when the person I showed asked if I could make them one as well. That happened for quite a few projects, especially the "Music for a Sushi Restaurant" Sushi, and the "Sunflower, Vol. 6" Bucket Hat. But some of my personal favorites are the "Falling" Patchwork Pullover and the "Fine Line" Butterfly Tattoo Blanket. I will also 100 percent be wearing the "Sweet Creature" Sheep Vest at every available opportunity, along with the "Two Ghosts" Slippers. And I have already made room on my bed for the *Harry's House* Pillow and the "Treat People with Kindness" Pillow of course!

I hope you find some favorites here as well; there are so many amazing ones to choose from. I can't wait to see them! Happy crocheting, friends.

Helpful Information

Here are some things to keep in mind while stitching the patterns in this book. At the back of the book, you'll find a glossary of crochet stitches and techniques with photographs you can refer to if you're a beginner or are unfamiliar with a term.

Skill Levels

(1) Basic: Projects use basic stitches and may include increases and decreases.

(2) Easy: Projects may include simple stitch patterns, color work, and/or shaping.

(3) Intermediate: Projects may include involved stitch patterns, color work, and/or shaping.

(4) Complex: Projects may include complex stitch patterns, color work, and/or shaping, using a variety of techniques and stitches simultaneously.

Abbreviations

beg = begin(ning)(s)
BLO = back loop only
C2C = corner to corner
ch = chain
dc2tog = double crochet 2 together
dc = double crochet
FLO = front loop only
hdc = half double crochet
hdc2tog = half double crochet 2 together
hdc3tog = half double crochet 3 together
inv-dec = invisible decrease
rep = repeat
rnd(s) = round(s)
RS = right side
sc = single crochet
sc2tog = single crochet 2 stitches together
sc3tog = single crochet 3 stitches together
sk = skip
sl st = slip stitch
st(s) = stitch(es)
tr = treble crochet
WS = wrong side
yo = yarn over

Term Conversions

Crochet techniques are the same universally, and everyone uses the same terms. However, US patterns and UK patterns are different because the terms denote different stitches. Here is a conversion chart to explain the differences.

US	UK
single crochet (sc)	double crochet (dc)
half double crochet (hdc)	half treble crochet (htr)
double crochet (dc)	treble crochet (tr)
treble crochet (tr)	double treble crochet (dtr)
skip (sk)	miss
yarn over (yo)	yarn over hook (yoh)

Checking Your Gauge

Every pattern will tell you the exact yarn (or weight of yarn) to use and what size hook to use to crochet an item with the same finished measurements as the project shown. It is important to choose yarn in the weight specified in order to successfully complete the project. The hook size recommended is the size an average crocheter would use to get the correct gauge. Gauge refers to the number of stitches and the number of rows in a given width and length, usually in 4" (10 cm) of crocheted fabric.

We can't all be average. Some of us crochet tighter, others looser. Before beginning to crochet a project, it is very important to take the time to check your gauge. Start by making a chain a little over 4" (10 cm) long, and then work the pattern stitch, using the yarn and hook called for in the instructions, until you have an approximate 4" (10 cm) square. Most crocheters do not get accurate row gauges because of the differences in how the stitch loop is picked up, so it is more accurate to check your gauge by the stitch count rather than row count.

14 UNOFFICIAL HARRY STYLES CROCHET

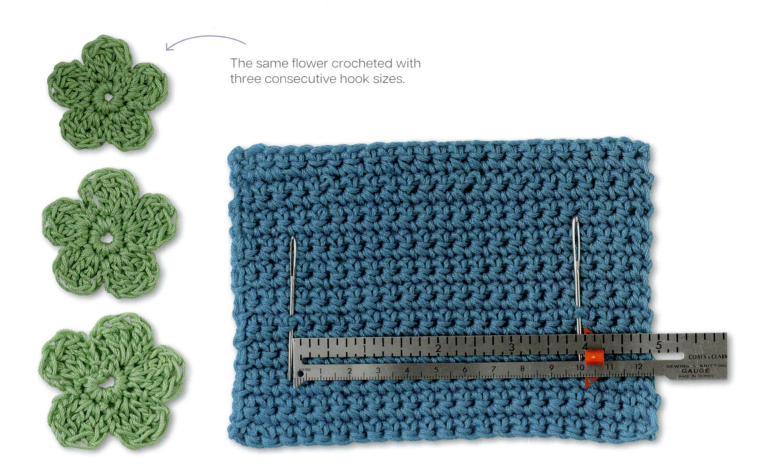

The same flower crocheted with three consecutive hook sizes.

Place a pin on one side of the work, and place another pin 4" (10 cm) over. Count the stitches between the pins. If you have more stitches to the inch than the instructions call for, you are working tighter than average; try a new swatch with a larger hook. If you have fewer stitches to the inch than the instructions call for, you are working looser than average; try a smaller hook.

Note

It is better to change hook size to get proper gauge, rather than trying to work tighter or looser. Usually the gauge stated means "as worked." In some instances, a pattern will give measurements of a garment "after blocking." This means that after an item is blocked, it will stretch a little.

Hook Sizes

Metric Size	US Size
2.25 mm	B/1
2.75 mm	C/2
3.25 mm	D/3
3.5 mm	E/4
3.75 mm	F/5
4 mm	G/6
4.5 mm	7
5 mm	H/8
5.5 mm	I/9
6 mm	J/10
6.5 mm	K/10½
8 mm	L/11
9 mm	M/N/13
10 mm	N/P/15
15 mm	P/Q
16 mm	Q
19 mm	S

HELPFUL INFORMATION

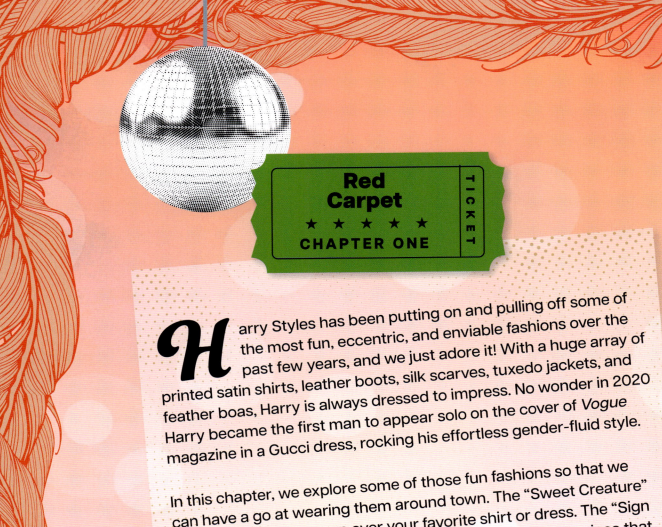

Red Carpet
CHAPTER ONE

Harry Styles has been putting on and pulling off some of the most fun, eccentric, and enviable fashions over the past few years, and we just adore it! With a huge array of printed satin shirts, leather boots, silk scarves, tuxedo jackets, and feather boas, Harry is always dressed to impress. No wonder in 2020 Harry became the first man to appear solo on the cover of *Vogue* magazine in a Gucci dress, rocking his effortless gender-fluid style.

In this chapter, we explore some of those fun fashions so that we can have a go at wearing them around town. The "Sweet Creature" Sheep Vest can be worn over your favorite shirt or dress. The "Sign of the Times" Black Lace Shawl is an absolutely stunning piece that evokes the black lace outfit that Harry stepped out in and can be worn draped over your shoulders or as a neck wrap. The "Golden" Cardigan is a cozy number perfect for those cool autumn days. And for warmer outings, pair the "Adore You" Strawberry Halter with the "Cherry" Earrings for the perfect summer look!

"If all I get is to make this music, I'm content. If I'm never on that big ride again, I'm happy and proud of it."

Skill Level 1 2 3 4

"Sweet Creature" Sheep Vest

Designed by Lee Sartori

"Sweet Creature" is a pretty and wistful lullaby about the common bond between two people and the home they share together. It's about the strength of the connection that young love brings and the warmth that they experience together despite everything going on around them. No matter what happens, they are two hearts yearning to be together.

Size
XS (S, M, L, 1X, 2X, 3X, 4X, 5X)

Measurements
To fit bust: 28–30 (32–34, 36–38, 40–42, 44–46, 48–50, 52–54, 56–58, 60–62)" [71–76 (81.5–86.5, 91.5–96.5, 101.5–106.5, 112–117, 122–127, 132–137, 142–147.5, 152.5–157.5) cm]

Finished chest: 32 (36, 40, 44, 48, 52, 56, 60, 64)" [81.5 (91.5, 101.5, 112, 122, 132, 142, 152.5, 162.5) cm]

Finished length: 20 (20, 21, 21, 22, 22, 22, 23, 23)" [51 (51, 53.5, 53.5, 56, 56, 56, 58.5, 58.5) cm]

Yarn
Worsted weight (#4 Medium)

Shown here: Lion Brand Basic Stitch Anti-Pilling, 185 yds (170 m), 3½ oz (100 g), 100% acrylic: 3 (3, 3, 4, 4, 4, 5, 5, 5) balls 406N Deep Denim Heather (A), 1 ball each 153 Black (B), 100 White (C).

Hook
US Size G/6 (4 mm) crochet hook. Adjust hook size if necessary to obtain correct gauge.

Notions
Yarn needle

Scissors

Gauge
18 sc x 20 rows = 4" (10 cm) in sc worked in rows

Notes
♥ Vest is worked in two panels that are seamed at the shoulders and sides.

♥ The front panel features color work, and the back panel is plain.

♥ To change yarn color, draw new color through the last yarn over of previous stitch.

♥ Carry colors not in use along back of panel, stitch over the top of the carried strand every 5 stitches to avoid long floats.

CONTINUED

CHAPTER ONE: RED CARPET

BACK PANEL

Lower Ribbing

With A.

Row 1: Ch 6, sc in 2nd ch from hook and in each ch across, turn—5 sc.

Rows 2–72 (81, 91, 99, 108, 118, 126, 135, 145): Ch 1, sc in BLO of each st across, turn.

Body

With A.

Rotate to work across row ends of Hem.

Row 1: Ch 1, sc in each row end across, turn—72 (81, 91, 99, 108, 118, 126, 135, 145) sc.

Rows 2–60: Ch 1, sc in each st across, turn.

Fasten off.

Row 61 (Arm Indent): Skip next 10 sts, rejoin in next st with a sl st, ch 1, sc in same st and in each st across to last 10 sts, leave remaining 10 sts unworked, turn—52 (61, 71, 79, 88, 98, 106, 115, 125) sc.

Rows 62–86 (86, 91, 91, 96, 96, 96, 101, 101): Ch 1, sc in each st across, turn.

Left Shoulder

Row 1: Ch 1, sc in next 8 (8, 13, 17, 21, 26, 30, 35, 40) sts, turn leaving remaining sts unworked—8 (8, 13, 17, 21, 26, 30, 35, 40) sts.

Rows 2–10: Ch 1, sc in each st across, turn.

Fasten off, leaving a long tail for sewing.

Right Shoulder

Row 1: Skip center 36 (45, 45, 45, 46, 46, 46, 45, 45) sts for neckline and join in next st, ch 1, sc in same st and in each st across, turn—8 (8, 13, 17, 21, 26, 30, 35, 40) sts.

Rows 2–10: Ch 1, sc in each st across, turn.

Fasten off, leaving a long tail for sewing.

COLOR CHART

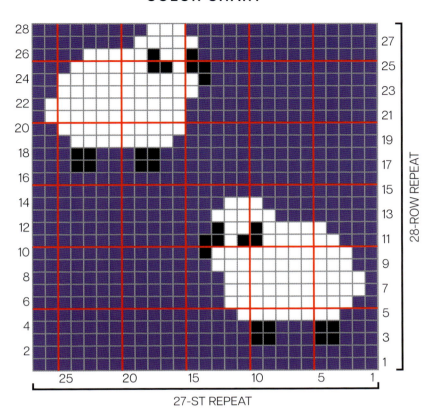

KEY
- Deep Denim Heather (A)
- ■ Black (B)
- ☐ White (C)

28-ROW REPEAT
27-ST REPEAT

FRONT PANEL

Follow the color chart provided to complete the Front Panel. The color chart is a 27-st by 28-row repeat, so the 1st row of the chart will repeat several times across your panel depending on the size. For example, the size S has 3 repeats of Row 1 of the chart across before moving to Row 2 of the chart.

Hem

With A.

Row 1: Ch 6, sc in 2nd ch from hook and in each ch across, turn—5 sc.

Rows 2–72 (81, 91, 99, 108, 118, 126, 135, 145): Ch 1, sc in BLO of each st across, turn.

Body

With A.

Rotate to work across row ends of Hem.

Row 1: Ch 1, sc in each row end across, turn—72 (81, 91, 99, 108, 118, 126, 135, 145) sc.

The remaining rows may have side stitches added to ensure a complete repeat of the color chart. If your size has "0," there are no side stitches needed, and you can proceed with the color chart. Complete side stitches in color A.

Row 2: With A, ch 1, sc in first 9 (0, 5, 9, 0, 5, 9, 0, 5); sc in each st AND change yarn color following Row 2 of chart to last 9 (0, 5, 9, 0, 5, 9, 0, 5) sts; with A, sc in each st to end of row, turn.

Rows 3–60: With A, ch 1, sc in first 9 (0, 5, 9, 0, 5, 9, 0, 5); sc in each st AND change yarn color following next row of chart to last 9 (0, 5, 9, 0, 5, 9, 0, 5) sts; with A, sc in each st to end of row, turn.

→ CONTINUED

CHAPTER ONE: RED CARPET

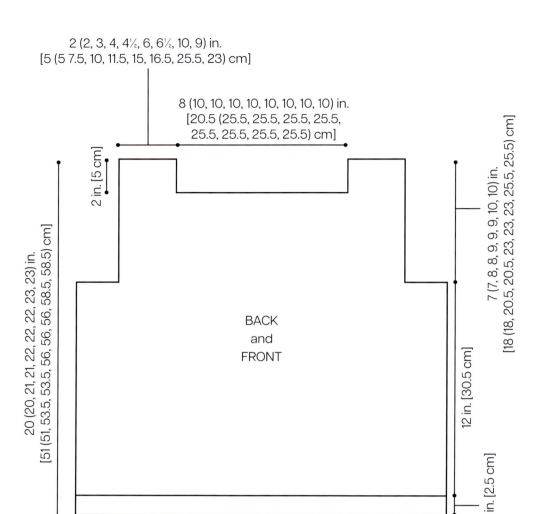

SCHEMATIC

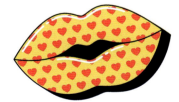

"PEOPLE JUST WANT ME TO BE MYSELF AND BE AUTHENTIC WITH THEM."

The following rows will affect how you read the color chart due to skipped stitches for the Arm Indent.

Continue changing yarn color following chart, and line up the sheep of the color chart with the corresponding sheep in previous rows.

Row 61 (Arm Indent): Skip next 10 sts, rejoin in next st with a sl st, ch 1, sc in same st and in each st across to last 10 sts, leave remaining 10 sts unworked, turn—52 (61, 71, 79, 88, 98, 106, 115, 125) sc.

Rows 62–86 (86, 91, 91, 96, 96, 96, 101, 101): Ch 1, sc in each st across, turn.

Right Shoulder

Continue lining up the sheep of the color chart with the corresponding sheep in previous rows.

Row 1: Ch 1, sc in next 8 (8, 13, 17, 21, 26, 30, 35, 40) sts, turn leaving remaining sts unworked—8 (8, 13, 17, 21, 26, 30, 35, 40) sts.

Rows 2–10: Ch 1, sc in each st across, turn.

Fasten off, leaving a long tail for sewing.

Left Shoulder

Continue lining up the sheep of the color chart with the corresponding sheep in previous rows

Row 1: Skip center 36 (45, 45, 45, 46, 46, 46, 45, 45) sts for neckline and join in next st, ch 1, sc in same st and in each st across, turn—8 (8, 13, 17, 21, 26, 30, 35, 40) sts.

Rows 2–10: Ch 1, sc in each st across, turn.

Fasten off, leaving a long tail for sewing.

FINISHING

With WS facing, seam shoulder seams. Seam sides from Arm Indent to Hem. Weave in ends.

Collar Trim

With A.

Rnd 1: Sl st to back edge of vest, ch 1, sc in each st and row-end evenly around entire neckline, join.

Fasten off, weave in ends.

Armhole Trim

With A.

Rnd 1: Sl st to any st around armhole opening, ch 1, sc in each st and row-end evenly around entire arm hole, join.

Fasten off, weave in ends.

Rep for opposite arm hole.

Style Like Styles

By changing the main color of the "Sweet Creature" Sheep Vest, you can change the entire look! Choose your favorite color for the background, and make your sheep pop!

CHAPTER ONE: RED CARPET

"As It Was" Harry Styles Doll

Designed by Lee Sartori

Skill Level

Is "As It Was" an introvert anthem? Maybe! As an introverted extrovert, I can definitely relate to the feelings of being no good alone, and yet I spend so much of my time crocheting and listening to audiobooks by myself. This song is filled with the nostalgic feelings of wanting to experience everything but also wanting to curl up on your couch with a good crochet project and turn off the world outside. Whether you are an introvert or an extrovert, it's important to take care and to allow others in to take care as well!

The "As It Was" Harry Styles Doll features Harry's outfit from the music video, his fire-engine-red jumpsuit. Feel free to add a little black feather boa around his neck if you have some scrap fun-fur yarn!

Measurements

14" (35.5 cm) tall

Yarn

Worsted weight (#4 Medium)

Shown here: Lion Brand Basic Stitch Anti-Pilling, 185 yds (170 m), 3½ oz (100 g), 100% acrylic: 1 ball each 121L Almond (A), 153 Black (B), 126AL Mahogany (D)

Shown here: Lion Brand Vanna's Choice, 170yds (156 m), 3½ oz (100 g), 100% acrylic: 1 ball 113 Scarlet (C)

Hook

US Size D/3 (3.25 mm) crochet hook. Adjust hook size if necessary to obtain correct gauge.

Notions

Fiberfill

1 pair of 12 mm black safety eyes

White felt

Black fine tip marker

Red sparkle ribbon approximately ½" (13 mm) wide

Yarn needle

Stitch marker

Scissors

Gauge

Gauge is not critical for this project.

24 sc x 26 rows = 4" (10 cm)

Notes

♥ The doll is worked bottom up, with arms made separately and added in as the body progresses.

Special Stitches

Hdc2tog (half double crochet 2 together): Yo and insert hook in indicated st, yo and draw up a loop, yo and insert hook into next st, yo draw up a loop, yo and draw through all loops on hook.

Hdc3tog (half double crochet 3 together): Yo and insert hook in indicated st, yo and draw up a loop, [yo and insert hook into next st, yo and draw up a loop] twice, yo and draw through all loops on hook.

Inv-dec (invisible single crochet decrease): Insert hook in FLO of each of next 2 sts, yo and draw through both sts, yo and draw through 2 loops on hook—1 st decreased.

CONTINUED

CHAPTER ONE: RED CARPET

ARM (MAKE 2)

With A.

Rnd 1: Ch 5, beg in 2nd ch from hook, sc in next 3 ch, 3 sc in next ch, rotate to work on the underside of foundation ch, sc in next 3 ch, 3 sc in last ch (this is the ch that was skipped at the beg of this rnd)—12 sc.

Place marker in last sc made to indicate end of rnd. Move marker up as each rnd is completed.

Rnd 2: Sc in next 4 sts, 2 sc in next st, sc in next 5 sts, 2 sc in next st, sc in last st—14 sc.

Rnd 3: Sc in each st around.

Rnd 4: Sc in next 6 sts, ch 3, 3 sc in 2nd ch from hook (*thumb made*), sc in next ch, sc in next 8 sts—18 sc.

Rnd 5: Sc in next 6 sts, skip 4 sc of thumb, sc in next 8 sts—14 sc.

Rnd 6: [Sc in next 5 sts, inv-dec] twice—12 sc.

Stuff hand, continue stuffing arm as work progresses.

Rnd 7: [Sc in next 4 sts, inv-dec] twice—10 sc.

Rnds 8–22: Sc in each st around.

Fasten off, set aside to join to Body at indicated rnd.

SHOES (MAKE 2 PIECES FOR EACH SHOE)

With B.

Rnd 1: Ch 9, sc in 2nd ch from hook, sc in next 6 ch, 3 sc in next ch, rotate to work on the underside of foundation ch, sc in next 7 ch, 3 sc in last ch—20 sc.

Place marker in last sc made to indicate end of rnd. Move marker up as each rnd is completed.

Rnd 2: Sc in next 7 sts, 2 sc in each of next 3 sts, sc in next 8 sts, 3 sc in next st, sc in last st—25 sc.

Rnd 3: Sc in next 7 sts, [2 sc in next st, sc in next st] 3 times, sc in next 9 sts, 3 sc in next st, sc in last 2 sts—30 sc.

Fasten off 1st piece, do not fasten off 2nd piece.

Rnd 4: With 2 pieces atop one another and working through both thicknesses, sc in each st around—30 sc.

Rnd 5: Sc in next 7 sts, [sc in next st, inv-dec] 3 times, sc in next 14 sts—27 sc.

Rnd 6: Sc in next 7 sts, inv-dec, [hdc2tog] twice, inv-dec, sc in next 12 sts—23 sts.

Rnd 7: Sc in next st, [inv-dec] 3 times, [hdc3tog] twice, [inv-dec] 3 times, sc in next 2 sts, inv-dec—12 sts.

Fasten off, stuff the shoe. Do not overstuff.

UNOFFICIAL HARRY STYLES CROCHET

CHAPTER ONE: RED CARPET

Rnd 11: Sc in each st around, do not join.

Rnd 12: Sc in next 3 sts, [sc in next st, 2 sc in next st] 4 times, sc in next 4 sts—19 sc.

Rnd 13: Sc in next 5 sts, inv-dec, [2 sc in next st, sc in next st] 3 times, 2 sc in next st, inv-dec, sc in next 3 sts—21 sc.

Rnd 14: Sc in next 6 sts, [inv-dec] 6 times, sc in next 3 sts—15 sc.

Rnd 15: [Sc in next 4 sts, 2 sc in next st] around—18 sc.

Rnd 16: [Sc in next 5 sts, 2 sc in next st] around—21 sc.

Rnd 17: [Sc in next 6 sts, 2 sc in next st] around—24 sc.

Rnds 18–25: Sc in each st around.

Fasten off. Stuff legs.

LEG (MAKE 2)

Join C to back of heel.

Rnds 1–5: Ch 1, sc in each st around; join with a sl st to 1st st—12 sc.

Rnd 6: Ch 1, sc in next 11 sts, 2 sc in last st, join—13 sc.

Rnd 7: Ch 1, sc in next 12 sts, 2 sc in last st, join—14 sc.

Rnd 8: Ch 1, sc in next 13 sts, 2 sc in last st, join—15 sc.

Rnds 9 and 10: Ch 1, sc in each st around, join.

BODY

With C.

With back of Legs facing, mark st in middle of each inner thigh where legs will join.

Rnd 1: With back of Legs facing and beg in marked st, sc in 24 sts around 1st leg, ch 3, sc in marked st of 2nd leg, sc in each st around—48 sc, ch-3.

Place marker in last sc made to indicate end of rnd. Move marker up as each rnd is completed.

"'As It Was' is about metamorphosis, embracing change and former self, perspective shift and all that kind of stuff. It just felt like the thing I wanted to say, the thing I wanted to be doing and the kind of music I wanted to make coming back." —Harry Styles

Rnd 2: Sc in each of next 3 ch, sc in next 24 sts, sc in underside of next 3 ch, sc in next 24 sts—54 sc.

Rnd 3: 2 sc in next st, 3 sc in next st, 2 sc in next 2 sts, sc in each st around to last st, 2 sc in last st—60 sc.

Rnds 4–12: Sc in each st around.

Rnd 13: Sc in next 4 sts, sc3tog, sc in next 4 sts, sc3tog, sc in each st around to last 3 sts, sc3tog—54 sc.

Rnds 14–23: Sc in each st around.

Incorporate arms into next round.

Rnd 24: With C, sc in next 19 sts; with A, sc in next 10 sts around Left Arm ensuring that thumb is facing body; continuing with C, sc in next 27 sts; with A, sc in next 10 sts around Right Arm ensuring that thumb is facing body; with C, sc in next 8 sts—74 sc.

Fasten off C, continue with A.

Rnd 25: Sc in next 23 sts, inv-dec, sc in next 35 sts, inv-dec, sc in next 12 sts—72 sc.

Rnd 26: [Sc in next 10 sts, inv-dec] around—66 sc.

Rnd 27: [Sc in next 9 sts, inv-dec] around—60 sc.

Stuff arms and body, continue stuffing as work progresses.

Rnd 28: [Sc in next 8 sts, inv-dec] around—54 sc.

Rnd 29: [Sc in next 7 sts, inv-dec] around—48 sc.

Rnd 30: [Sc in next 6 sts, inv-dec] around—42 sc.

Rnd 31: [Sc in next 5 sts, inv-dec] around—36 sc.

Rnd 32: [Sc in next 4 sts, inv-dec] around—30 sc.

Rnd 33: [Sc in next 3 sts, inv-dec] around—24 sc.

Rnd 34: [Sc in next 2 sts, inv-dec] around—18 sc.

Rnd 35: Sc in each st around.

Finish stuffing, paying close attention to stuffing tops of arms/shoulders firmly.

HEAD

With A.

Rnd 1: Working in BLO of last rnd of Body, sc in each st around—18 sc.

Place marker in last sc made to indicate end of rnd. Move marker up as each rnd is completed.

Rnd 2: 2 sc in each st around—36 sc.

Rnd 3: [Sc in next 5 sts, 2 sc in next st] around—42 sc.

Rnd 4: [Sc in next 3 sts, 2 sc in next st, sc in next 3 sts] around—48 sc.

Rnd 5: [Sc in next 7 sts, 2 sc in next st] around—54 sc.

Rnd 6: [Sc in next 4 sts, 2 sc in next st, sc in next 4 sts] around—60 sc.

Rnd 7: [Sc in next 9 sts, 2 sc in next st] around—66 sc.

Rnds 8–21: Sc in each st around.

Insert eyes in between Rnds 15 and 16, 12 sts apart. Before adding the safety backing, use white felt to add white detail to lower lid of eye. Using A, add nose detail between Rnds 12 and 13 over 3 sts. Using a length of A, cinch the eyes together by sewing a line between both eyes and pulling the line taught to create a slight dent.

Rnd 22: [Sc in next 9 sts, inv-dec] around—60 sc.

Rnd 23: [Sc in next 4 sts, inv-dec, sc in next 4 sts] around—54 sc.

Rnd 24: [Sc in next 7 sts, inv-dec] around—48 sc.

Rnd 25: [Sc in next 3 sts, inv-dec, sc in next 3 sts] around—42 sc.

Stuff Head and continue stuffing as work progresses.

Rnd 26: [Sc in next 5 sts, inv-dec] around—36 sc.

Rnd 27: [Sc in next 2 sts, inv-dec, sc in next 2 sts] around—30 sc.

Rnd 28: [Sc in next 3 sts, inv-dec] around—24 sc.

Rnd 29: [Sc in next st, inv-dec, sc in next st] around—18 sc.

Rnd 30: [Sc in next st, inv-dec] around—12 sc.

Rnd 31: Inv-dec around—6 sc.

Fasten off, leaving a long tail for sewing, sew remaining 6 sts closed. Weave in ends.

SHOULDER STRAPS (MAKE 2)

With C.

Row 1: Ch 17, working in the back bumps of ch, sc in 2nd ch from the hook and in each ch across—16 sc.

Fasten off, leaving a long tail for sewing. Sew Shoulder Straps to top edges of jumpsuit. Weave in ends.

EARS (MAKE 2)

With A.

Row 1: Ch 2, (3 sc, 3 hdc, sl st) in 2nd ch from hook—7 sts.

Fasten off, leaving a long tail for sewing.

HAIR CROWN

With D, work in BLO for entire piece.

Rnd 1: Ch 2, 6 sc in 2nd ch from hook—6 sc.

Place marker in last sc made to indicate end of rnd. Move marker up as each rnd is completed.

Rnd 2: 2 sc in each st around—12 sc.

Rnd 3: [2 sc in next st, sc in next st] around—18 sc.

Rnd 4: [Sc in next st, 2 sc in next st, sc in next st] around—24 sc.

Rnd 5: [2 sc in next st, sc in next 3 sts] around—30 sc.

Rnd 6: [Sc in next 2 sts, 2 sc in next st, sc in next 2 sts] around—36 sc.

Rnd 7: [2 sc in next st, sc in next 5 sts] around—42 sc.

Rnd 8: [Sc in next 3 sts, 2 sc in next st, sc in next 3 sts] around—48 sc.

Rnd 9: [2 sc in next st, sc in next 7 sts] around—54 sc.

Rnd 10: [Sc in next 4 sts, 2 sc in next st, sc in next 4 sts] around—60 sc.

Rnd 11: [2 sc in next st, sc in next 9 sts] around—66 sc.

Rnds 12–14: Sc in each st around.

Begin working in turned rows.

Row 15: Working in BLO, sc in next 48 sts, turn leaving remaining 18 sts unworked—48 sc.

Row 16: Ch 1, skip 1st st, working in FLO across, sc in next 45 sts, inv-dec, turn—45 sc.

Row 17: Ch 1, skip 1st st, working in BLO across, sc in next 42 sts, inv-dec, turn leaving last st unworked—43 sc.

Row 18: Ch 1, skip 1st st, working in FLO across, sc in next 40 sts, inv-dec, turn—41 sc.

Fasten off, leaving a long tail for sewing. Sew Hair Crown to top of Head with 18 sts of Row 15 set at forehead, 7 rnds above edge of safety eyes. Sew Ears to each side of Head over edge of Hair Crown. Weave in ends.

BANGS (MAKE 3)

With D.

Row 1: Ch 13, working in the back bumps of the ch, sc in 2nd ch from hook and in each ch across—12 sc.

Fasten off, leaving a long tail for sewing. Sew the 3 bangs to the very center of the forehead, looping 2 strands back and leaving 1 strand hanging above the right eyebrow.

FINISHING

Using photos as a guide, secure ribbon to jumpsuit in diamond pattern. Using photos as a guide, use black marker to draw tattoos on body and arms.

"Sign of the Times" Black Lace Shawl

Designed by Krysten Grymes

Skill Level 1 2 3 4

Finding your own voice can be the catalyst for huge change in your life. Speaking up, speaking out, and finding authenticity is so freeing! For Harry Styles, finding his honest voice came with the song "Sign of the Times." "I think I've always written bits of songs alone, and then I usually take stuff in and try to finish it with someone," Harry explained. "'Sign of the Times' was one of those where I just kind of wrote it. We basically ended up in a place where the album had a bunch of rock songs and a bunch of acoustic, kind of picked ballad songs. And I wrote 'Sign of the Times' and just felt like there was all this middle ground that I wanted to then explore. And I think that's the one that kind of started bridging us to different places in terms of experimenting a little more." The "Sign of the Times" Black Lace Shawl is a nod to the Gucci sheer blouse that Harry Styles wore to the 2019 Met Gala. It's such an amazing look, we couldn't resist matching it to the perfect lacy shawl pattern to bring it to life! This shawl is made by joining individual crochet circles that are then assembled so that a border can be added. Finish it off with some gorgeous draping tassels, and get ready to wear it on a night out!

Size
One size fits most

Measurements
Finished wingspan: 70" (178 cm)

Finished length: 35" (90 cm)

Yarn
DK weight (#3 Light)

Shown here: Lion Brand 100% Superwash Merino, 306 yds (280 m), 3½ oz (100 g): 3 balls 153K Night Sky

Hook
US H/8 (5 mm) crochet hook. Adjust hook size if necessary to obtain correct gauge.

Notions
Yarn needle

Stitch marker

Scissors

Gauge
Small Circle: 2.75" x 2.75" (7 x 7 cm)

Large Circle: 6" x 6" (15 x 15 cm)

Half Circle: 6" x 3" (15 x 7.5 cm)

Notes

- ♥ The Shawl is made up of 36 small circles, 30 large circles, and 10 half circles.
- ♥ The circles are joined together using a "join as you go" method to form the Shawl.
- ♥ Tassels are attached to the completed Shawl.

CONTINUED

CHAPTER ONE: RED CARPET

33

Special Stitches

Use the following "join as you go" (JAYG) method to join your circles together. You will use this method on the final round of each circle.

Work the final round of the circle as instructed. Once you reach the stitch where you will join the circle to the neighboring circle, before completing the stitch, do the following:

1. Remove the loop of yarn from your hook and locate the stitch on the neighboring circle where you plan to place the join.
2. Insert the hook underneath the front and back loop of the stitch. Place the loop of the working circle back onto the hook. Draw up a loop.
3. Work the next stitch on the working circle as instructed.
4. Continue working in pattern until you reach the next place you'd like to place a join.

Repeat steps 1–3.

SMALL CIRCLE (MAKE 36)

Rnd 1: Make a magic circle, ch 1 (counts as first sc), 15 sc in circle; join with sl st in beg ch-1—16 sts.

Pull beginning tail to cinch circle closed—16 sts.

Rnd 2: Ch 3 (counts as hdc, ch 1), hdc in next sc, [ch 1, hdc in next sc] 14 times, ch 1; join with sl st in 2nd ch of beg ch-3—32 sts.

Rnd 3: Ch 1, work 1 sc in each ch-1 space and hdc around; join with sl st in beg ch-1.

Fasten off.

LARGE CIRCLE (MAKE 30)

Rnds 1–3: Work same as Rnds 1–3 of Small Circle—32 sts.

Rnd 4: Ch 5 (counts as dc, ch 2), skip next st, dc in next st, [ch 2, skip next st, dc in next st] 14 times, ch 2; join with sl st in 3rd ch of beg ch-5—16 dc, 16 ch-2 spaces.

Rnd 5: Ch 1, work 2 sc in each ch-2 space and 1 sc in each dc around; join with sl st in beg ch-1—48 sc.

Rnd 6: Ch 7 (counts as dc, ch 4), skip next 2 sts, dc in next st, [ch 4, skip next 2 sts, dc in next st] 14 times, ch 4; join with sl st in 3rd st from beg, ch-7—16 dc, 16 ch-4 spaces.

Rnd 7: Ch 1, work 5 sc in each ch-4 space and 1 sc in each dc around; join with sl st in beg ch-1—96 sc.

Fasten off.

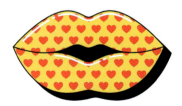

"'Sign of the Times,' for me, it's looking at several different things. . . . It's a time when it's very easy to feel incredibly sad about a lot of things. It's also nice sometimes to remember that while there's a lot of bad stuff, there's also a lot of amazing people doing amazing things in the world."

— Harry Styles

Style Like Styles

This shawl can be worn two ways! Drape it around your shoulders, or wear it around your neck with the shawl looped in the front for a completely different look!

CHAPTER ONE: RED CARPET

CONTINUED

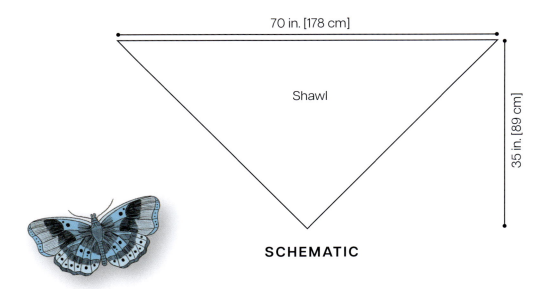

SCHEMATIC

HALF CIRCLE (MAKE 10)

The half circle is worked back and forth in rows.

Row 1: Make a magic circle, ch 1, 9 sc in circle, do not join, turn—9 sts.

Pull the beginning tail to cinch the circle closed.

Row 2: Ch 3 (counts as hdc, ch 1), hdc in next sc, [ch 1, hdc in next sc] 7 times, turn—9 hdc, 8 ch-1 spaces.

Row 3: Ch 1, sc in each ch-1 space and hdc across, turn—17 sc.

Row 4: Ch 5 (counts as dc, ch 2), skip next st, dc in next st, [ch 2, skip next st, dc in next st] 7 times, turn—9 dc, 8 ch-2 spaces.

Row 5: Ch 1, 2 sc in each ch-2 space and 1 sc in each dc across, turn—25 sc.

Row 6: Ch 7 (counts as dc, ch 4), skip next 2 sts, dc in next st, [ch 4, skip next 2 sts, dc in next st] 7 times—9 dc, 8 ch-4 spaces.

Row 7: Ch 1, work 5 sc in each ch-4 space and 1 sc in each dc across, turn—49 sc.

Fasten off.

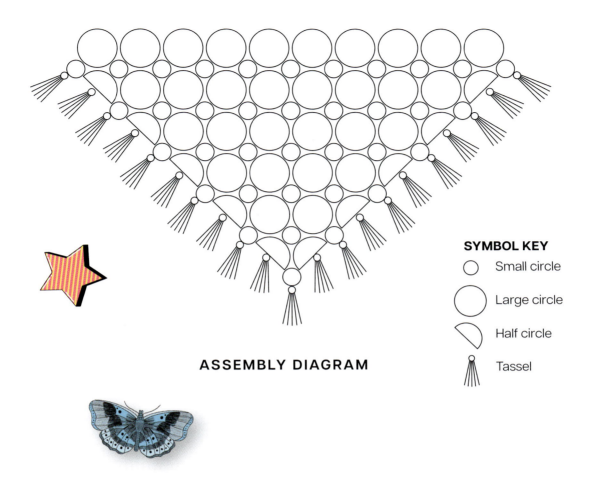

ASSEMBLY DIAGRAM

SYMBOL KEY
◯ Small circle
◯ Large circle
◗ Half circle
▼ Tassel

TASSELS (MAKE 21)

Cut twelve 8" (20.5 cm) pieces of yarn and one 10" (25.5 cm) piece.

You will attach the strands of yarn to the edge of the shawl using Larks Head Knots.

1. Working with 2 of the 8" (20.5 cm) pieces of yarn at a time, place them together and fold them in half to find the center.

2. Insert the crochet hook into a stitch of a circle or half circle on the bottom edges of the shawl. Draw a loop of the yarn through the stitch with the hook. Do not pull it all the way through.

3. Pull the tails of the yarn through the loop. Gently pull to cinch the loop closed and secure the 2 strands in place. Repeat steps 1–3 until all twelve of the 8" (20.5 cm) pieces are attached in different edge stitches of the same circle or half circle of the shawl.

4. Gather the attached yarn together and tie a knot using the 10" (25.5 cm) piece. Trim the ends of the strands to make them even.

Repeat steps 1–4 for all 21 tassels.

FINISHING

Secure and weave in all ends.

"Golden" Cardigan

Designed by Meghan Ballmer

"Golden" is an upbeat pop hit from Harry Styles's album *Fine Line*. Harry aimed to make a song to bring fun, and he did just that! Harry admitted the song, for him, has always been a source of joy, telling AP News, "I wanted to make a video that encapsulated that. I'd like to think it will maybe cheer a couple of people up. Cheered me up." The song is about the feeling of falling for someone when first seeing them and the fear that comes from not wanting to be alone. It's the happy bounce-back after heartbreak and the hope that things can only get better. The "Golden" Cardigan is a nod to those long drives along the coast with the sun straight ahead of you and nothing but happy memories being made. The back of the cardigan features a warm, glowing sun, and wearing it wraps you in that warmth that comes from crocheting something just for you!

Sizes
XS (S, M, L, XL, 2X, 3X, 4X, 5X)

Measurements
To fit bust: 35 (39, 43, 47, 51, 55, 59, 63, 67)" [89 (99, 109, 119.5, 129.5, 139.5, 150, 160, 170) cm]

Finished bust: 26½ (30½, 34½, 38½, 42½, 46½, 50½, 54½, 58½)" [67.5 (77.5, 87.5, 98, 108, 118, 128.5, 138.5, 148.5) cm], not including front bands

Finished length: 25 (25, 25, 25, 26, 26, 26, 26, 26)" [63.5 (63.5, 63.5, 63.5, 66, 66, 66, 66, 66) cm]

Yarn
DK weight (#3 Light)

Shown here: Lion Brand 100% Superwash Merino, 306 yds (280 m), 3½ oz (100 g): 4 (5, 5, 6, 7, 7, 8, 9, 9) balls 098K Antique (A), 1 ball 158Y Mustard Seed (B)

Hook
US Size F/4 (3.75 mm) crochet hook. Adjust hook size if necessary to obtain correct gauge.

Notions
Tapestry needle

Scissors

Gauge
20 sc FLO x 19 rows = 4" (10 cm)

Notes
- ♥ Cardigan is worked in five panels. All panels are worked bottom up starting with a ribbing.
- ♥ The back panel includes a color work section using tapestry crochet. A color chart is included.
- ♥ Collar is worked directly onto the cardigan after seaming.
- ♥ Chains at end of rows do not count as a stitch.

STYLE LIKE STYLES

The "Golden" Cardigan is so comfy! Make it one or two sizes bigger for an oversized look, and wrap yourself up in this cozy make!

CONTINUED

BACK PANEL

Ribbing

With A, ch 11.

Row 1: Sc BLO in 2nd ch from hook, sc in each ch across, ch 1, turn—10 sc.

Rows 2–87 (97, 107, 117, 127, 137, 147, 157, 167): Sc BLO in each st across, ch 1, turn—10 sc.

Turn piece 90 degrees and work the main body into the edge of the ribbing rows.

Main Body

Row 1 (RS): Sc in the end of each row of ribbing across, ch 1, turn—87 (97, 107, 117, 127, 137, 147, 157, 167) sc.

Rows 2–24 (24, 24, 24, 26, 26, 26, 26, 26): Sc FLO in each st across, ch 1, turn.

Sunshine Chart

Note: Use a combination of tapestry crochet and intarsia crochet, carrying the main color throughout and making sure any floats are on the WS of the sweater.

Continue to ch 1 and turn at the end of every row.

Row 1 (Setup Row–RS): With A, sc FLO in first 10 (15, 20, 25, 30, 35, 40, 45, 50) sts, sc FLO in next 67 sts AND change yarn color following Row 1 of Chart; with A, sc FLO in last 10 (15, 20, 25, 30, 35, 40, 45, 50) sts.

Continue to work in sc FLO and work first and last 10 (15, 20, 25, 30, 35, 40, 45, 50) sts with A and center 67 sts with yarn colors shown in next row of Chart, until all 69 rows of the Chart have been completed.

Fasten off B. Work remainder of Cardigan with A only.

Next 17 (17, 17, 17, 20, 20, 20, 20, 20) rows: Sc FLO in each st across, ch 1, turn—87 (97, 107, 117, 127, 137, 147, 157, 167) sc.

Fasten off, leaving a long tail for seaming.

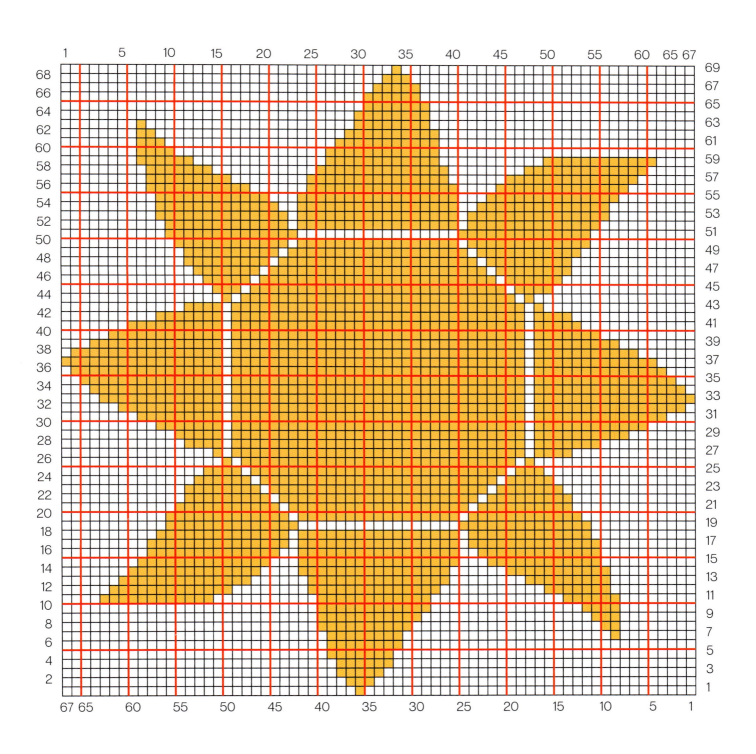

KEY

☐ Antique (A)
■ Mustard Seed (B)

SUNSHINE CHART

CHAPTER ONE: RED CARPET

FRONT PANELS (MAKE 2)

Ribbing

With A, ch 11.

Row 1: Sc BLO in 2nd ch from hook and in each ch across, ch 1, turn—10 sc.

Rows 2–23 (28, 33, 38, 43, 48, 53, 58, 63): Sc BLO in each st across, ch 1, turn.

Turn piece 90 degrees and work the main body into the edge of the ribbing rows.

Main Body

Row 1 (WS): Sc in the end of each row of ribbing across, ch 1, turn—23 (28, 33, 38, 43, 48, 53, 58, 63) sc.

Row 2–110 (110, 110, 110, 115, 115, 115, 115, 115): Sc FLO in each st across, ch 1, turn.

Fasten off, leaving a long tail for seaming.

SLEEVES (MAKE 2)

Ribbing

With A, ch 11.

Row 1: Sc BLO in 2nd ch from hook and in each ch across, ch 1, turn—10 sc.

Rows 2–40 (43, 43, 43, 45, 45, 48, 50, 53): Sc BLO in each st across, ch 1, turn.

Turn piece 90 degrees and work the first row of the sleeve into the edge of the ribbing rows.

Sleeve Body

Row 1: 2 sc in first end of row, sc in each end of row until one remains, 2 sc in last end of row, ch 1, turn—42 (45, 45, 45, 47, 47, 50, 52, 55) sc.

Next 4 (4, 3, 3, 2, 2, 2, 1, 1) row(s): Sc FLO in each st across, ch 1, turn.

Next row: 2 sc FLO in first st, sc FLO in each st across to last st, 2 sc FLO in last st, ch 1, turn—44 (47, 47, 47, 49, 49, 52, 54, 57) sc.

Rep these 5 (5, 4, 4, 3, 3, 3, 2, 2) rows 13 (13, 14, 17, 18, 21, 22, 23, 25) times—70 (73, 75, 81, 85, 91, 96, 100, 107) sts.

Next 5 (5, 15, 3, 14, 5, 0, 20, 11) rows: Sc FLO in each st across, ch 1, turn.

Fasten off, leaving a long tail for seaming.

"That's the amazing thing about music, there's a song for every emotion. Can you imagine a world with no music? It would suck and I'd still be a baker."

— Harry Styles

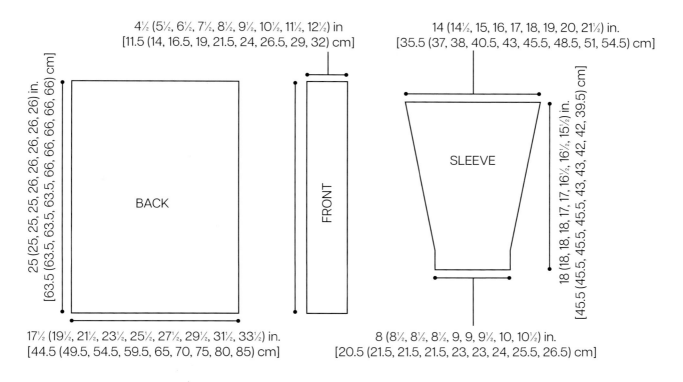

SCHEMATICS

SEAMING

Using a tapestry needle, seam the Front and Back Panels together at the shoulders using your preferred method of seaming. Then lay out the Front and Back Panels flat with RS facing up. Align each Sleeve along the edge of the Cardigan so that the center of the Sleeve is in line with the shoulder seam. I suggest using pins or stitch markers to hold the sleeve in place.

Starting at the shoulder seam and moving down along the Cardigan, seam the sleeve in place one side at a time.

Fold the Cardigan in half so the Sleeve and side edges are lined up. Then seam the sides and Sleeves using your preferred seaming method. It can be helpful to start at the underarm and work your way to the cuffs and bottom ribbing.

COLLAR

With RS facing out, attach MC yarn at bottom right ribbing.

Setup Row: Ch 1, sc in same st as join and in each st and end of row up the Front Right Panel, across the neckline and down the Front Left Panel, turn.

Row 1: Ch 11, sc in 2nd ch from hook and in each ch across, sl st in the next 2 sts of Setup Row, turn—10 sc, 2 sl sts.

Row 2: Sk sl sts, sc in BLO of each sc across, ch 1, turn—10 sc.

Row 3: Sc in BLO of each st across, sl st in next 2 sts of Setup Row, turn—10 sc, 2 sl sts.

Rep Rows 2 and 3 until you have gone along the entire Setup Row. Fasten off.

Weave in all ends. Block to measurements listed.

"Adore You" Strawberry Halter Top

Designed by Ashlee Elle

Adoration is such a strong feeling and one we designate for only the most special kind of people! I am lucky enough to have been with my partner for 16 years of marriage this year, and I can honestly say I adore him with all of my heart. "Adore You" by Harry Styles is a love song about feelings of lust and utter devotion. Its bubbly percussions and upbeat lyrics speak to the idea of wanting to love someone and the initial excitement of meeting someone new that sets a spark of passion alight. The beginning stages of a relationship can be so exciting, and the memories we make during those times can last a lifetime. The trendy "Adore You" Strawberry Halter Top is a nod to those perfect summer days with yummy drinks, sunglasses, and strawberry lipstick. Made with a strawberry motif in the center and surrounded by classic granny square stitches, this top is fun, approachable, and oh-so-wearable. Pair it with shorts, pants, or a skirt for the perfect look!

Size

XS/S (M, L/XL, 2X/3X, 4X/5X)

Measurements

Finished bust: 28 (32, 40, 46, 52)" [71 (81.5, 101.5, 117, 132) cm]

Finished length: 19" [48.5 cm]

Yarn

Worsted weight (#4 Medium)

Shown here: Lion Brand Basic Stitch Anti-Pilling, 185 yds (170 m), 3½ oz (100 g), 100% acrylic: 2 (3, 3, 4, 4) balls 100 White (A), 1 (1, 1, 2, 2) ball(s) 400G Red Heather (B), 1 (1, 1, 1, 1) ball 130B Grass (C)

Hook

US Size H/8 (5 mm) crochet hook. Adjust hook size if necessary to obtain correct gauge.

Notions

Stitch markers

Yarn needle

Scissors

Gauge

1 Granny Square = 6" x 6" (15 x 15 cm)

9 sts x 6 rows = 4" (10 cm) over Granny Rows pattern

Notes

- ♥ Halter is made from Granny Squares joined together following diagrams for front of Halter.
- ♥ Granny Rows are worked from side to side to form back of Halter, beginning on one side edge of front and working toward opposite side edge of front.
- ♥ Top and lower edgings and chain stitch straps are worked directly onto Halter.

CONTINUED

CHAPTER ONE: RED CARPET

GRANNY SQUARES (MAKE 7 [7, 9, 11, 11])

With B, ch 3; sl st in first ch to form a ring.

Strawberry

Rnd 1 (RS): Ch 2 (does not count as a st), work 11 hdc in ring; join with sl st in first hdc—11 hdc.

Rnd 2: Ch 1, (sc, hdc) in same st as joining sl st, 3 dc in next st, 2 dc in next st, 2 hdc in each of next 2 sts, 3 hdc in next st, 2 hdc in each of next 2 sts, 2 dc in next st, 3 dc in next st, hdc in last st; join with sl st in first sc—24 sts.

Rnd 3: Ch 1, sc in same st as joining sl st, 2 sc in each of next 3 sts, sc in next 8 sts, 3 hdc in next st, sc in next 8 sts, 2 sc in each of next 3 sts; join with sl st in first sc—32 sts.

Fasten off.

Outer Rnds

Rnd 4: With RS facing, draw up a loop of A in same st as joining sl st, ch 3 (counts as dc); working in back loops only, 2 dc in same st, ch 1, sk next 3 sts, (3 tr, ch 2, 3 tr) in next st, ch 1, sk next 2 sts, 3 hdc in next st, ch 1, sk next 3 sts, (3 dc, ch 2, 3 dc) in next st, ch 1, sk next 4 sts, 3 dc in next st, ch 1, sk next 4 sts, (3 dc, ch 2, 3 dc) in next st, ch 1, sk next 3 sts, 3 hdc in next st, ch 1, sk next 2 sts, (3 tr, ch 2, 3 tr) in next st, ch 1, sk next 3 sts; join with sl st in top of beg ch-3—39 sts, 8 ch-1 spaces, 4 ch-2 spaces.

Rnd 5: Ch 4 (counts as dc, ch 1), 3 dc in next ch-1 space, *ch 1, (3 dc, ch 2, 3 dc) in next ch-2 space, [ch 1, 3 dc in next ch-1 space] twice; rep from * 2 more times, ch 1, (3 dc, ch 2, 3 dc) in next ch-2 space, ch 1, 2 dc in last ch-1 space; join with sl st in 3rd ch of beg ch-4—16 3-dc groups, 8 ch-1 sps, 4 corner ch-2 sps (4 3-dc groups and 2 ch-1 sps along each of 4 sides between corner ch-2 sps).

Fasten off.

Leaves

With RS facing, join C with sl st in top center stitch of Strawberry.

Row 1: *Ch 5, sc in 2nd ch from hook and in next 3 ch (one leaf made); rep from * 2 more times—4 sc in each of 3 leaves.

Fasten off.

Seeds

With a length of A, embroider short straight sts randomly over Strawberry, beginning and ending on the back side of the Strawberry.

ASSEMBLE FRONT OF HALTER

Arrange Granny Squares following Layout Diagram. With A, sew Granny Squares together to form front of Halter.

BACK

With RS facing, draw up a loop of A in corner ch-2 space at the beginning of side edge of Front.

Granny Rows

Row 1: Ch 3 (counts as dc), 2 dc in same corner ch-2 space, *ch 1, 3 dc in next ch-space; rep from * all the way across to last corner ch-2 space of side edge, ch 1, dc in last corner ch-2 space.

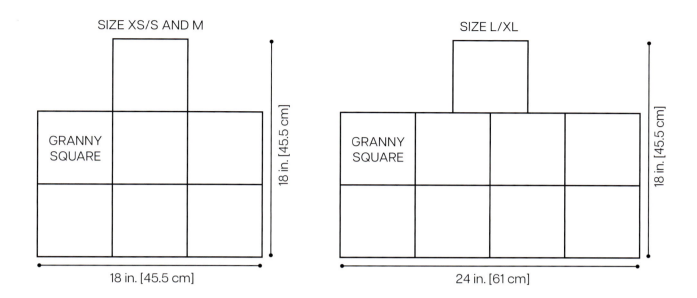
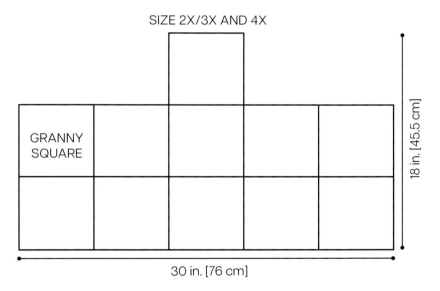

LAYOUT DIAGRAMS

Row 2: Ch 3 (counts as dc), 2 dc in first ch-1 space, *ch 1, 3 dc in next ch-space; rep from * to last 3-dc group, ch 1, dc in top of beg ch-3.

Rep Row 2 until entire piece (including Granny Square Front) measures about 28 (32, 40, 46, 52)" (71 (81.5, 101.5, 117, 132) cm), measured from side to side.

Fasten off, leaving a long yarn tail for sewing.

Sew last Granny Row to remaining side edge of Front.

FINISHING

Top Edging

With RS facing, draw up a loop of A in a space at center of back top edge.

Rnd 1: Ch 3 (counts as dc), 2 dc in same space, *ch 1, 3 dc in next space; rep from * working the ch 1 and 3-dc groups evenly spaced all the way around top edge of Halter; join with sl st in top of beg ch-3.

Rnd 2: Ch 2 (counts as hdc), hdc in each dc and ch-1 space around; join with sl st in top of beg ch-2.

Note: If a wider or taller front piece is desired, rep Rnd 2 (working hdc in each st around) until front piece is as wide and tall as desired.

Fasten off.

Lower Edging

With RS facing, draw up a loop of A anywhere in lower edge of Halter.

Rnd 1: Ch 1, work sc evenly spaced all the way around lower edge of Halter; join with sl st in first sc.

Fasten off.

Straps

First Strap: With RS facing, draw up a loop of A in beginning corner of top edge (center front Granny), ch 51.

Fasten off.

Second Strap: With RS facing, draw up a loop of A in ending corner of top edge (center front Granny), ch 51.

Fasten off.

Weave in any remaining ends. Block Halter, if desired.

STYLE LIKE STYLES

Halter tops look great on their own, but for a bit more coverage, wear it atop a tank top or a T-shirt for an equally cute look!

"Eventually someone's going to see that that's not who you are. So, it's best to be yourself from the get-go."

CHAPTER ONE: RED CARPET

"Watermelon Sugar" Clutch

Designed by Lee Sartori

You can't have a book inspired by Harry Styles and not include "Watermelon Sugar." But how do you describe this catchy but not-safe-for-work song? Especially after Harry Styles himself went on record to confirm it? Hmm . . . you could say that it evokes that "summer feeling"? You could say the song is very upbeat and happy sounding? You could also say that after watching the music video for "Watermelon Sugar," we will never look at a watermelon the same way again . . . (cough). In the end, it doesn't really matter what the song is about, we just know that we love it, and we love the vibe! You can crochet your own little "Watermelon Sugar" Clutch to carry around this summer! It's the perfect size to fit your small items and still be comfy! It's also very beginner friendly for our new crocheters out there! Add an optional zipper to close it, and be on your way to your next event!

Measurements

12" x 6" (30.5 cm x 15 cm)

Yarn

DK weight (#3 Light)

Shown here: Lion Brand Coboo, 232 yds (212 m), 3½ oz (100 g), 51% cotton/49% rayon from bamboo: 1 ball each 144L Magenta (A), 100 White (B), 132 Olive (C), 152R Coal (D).

Hook

US Size C/2 (2.5 mm) crochet hook. Adjust hook size if necessary to obtain correct gauge.

Notions

Purse strap

Black embroidery thread

Yarn needle

Scissors

Stitch marker

8" (20.5 cm) zipper (optional)

Gauge

Gauge is not critical to this project.

Rnds 1–14 = 4" (10 cm) diameter

Notes

♥ Purse is worked in one piece from the center outwards.

♥ Work in continuous rounds unless otherwise indicated.

♥ Ch 1 does not count as a stitch.

♥ Join by slip stitching in first stitch.

STYLE LIKE STYLES

Pair the "Watermelon Sugar" Clutch with the "Cherry" Earrings for a summer mix of perfect accessories!

CHAPTER ONE: RED CARPET

CONTINUED

CLUTCH

With A.

Rnd 1: Ch 2, work 6 sc in 2nd ch from hook—6 sc.

Rnd 2: 2 sc in each sc around—12 sc.

Rnd 3: [2 sc in next sc, sc in next sc] around—18 sc.

Rnd 4: [Sc in next sc, 2 sc in next sc, sc in next sc] around—24 sc.

Rnd 5: [2 sc in next sc, sc in next 3 sc] around—30 sc.

Rnd 6: [Sc in next 2 sc, 2 sc in next sc, sc in next 2 sc] around—36 sc.

Rnd 7: [2 sc in next sc, sc in next 5 sc] around—42 sc.

Rnd 8: [Sc in next 3 sc, 2 sc in next sc, sc in next 3 sc] around—48 sc.

Rnd 9: [2 sc in next sc, sc in next 7 sc] around—54 sc.

Rnd 10: [Sc in next 4 sc, 2 sc in next sc, sc in next 4 sc] around—60 sc.

Rnd 11: [2 sc in next sc, sc in next 9 sc] around—66 sc.

Rnd 12: [Sc in next 5 sc, 2 sc in next sc, sc in next 5 sc] around—72 sc.

Rnd 13: [2 sc in next sc, sc in next 11 sc] around—78 sc.

Rnd 14: [Sc in next 6 sc, 2 sc in next sc, sc in next 6 sc] around—84 sc.

Rnd 15: [2 sc in next sc, sc in next 13 sc] around—90 sc.

Rnd 16: [Sc in next 7 sc, 2 sc in next sc, sc in next 7 sc] around—96 sc.

Rnd 17: [2 sc in next sc, sc in next 15 sc] around—102 sc.

Rnd 18: [Sc in next 8 sc, 2 sc in next sc, sc in next 8 sc] around—108 sc.

Rnd 19: [2 sc in next sc, sc in next 17 sc] around—114 sc.

Rnd 20: [Sc in next 9 sc, 2 sc in next sc, sc in next 9 sc] around—120 sc.

Rnd 21: [2 sc in next sc, sc in next 19 sc] around—126 sc.

Rnd 22: [Sc in next 10 sc, 2 sc in next sc, sc in next 10 sc] around—132 sc.

Rnd 23: [2 sc in next sc, sc in next 21 sc] around—138 sc.

Rnd 24: [Sc in next 11 sc, 2 sc in next sc, sc in next 11 sc] around—144 sc.

Rnd 25: [2 sc in next sc, sc in next 23 sc] around—150 sc.

Rnd 26: [Sc in next 12 sc, 2 sc in next sc, sc 12 sc] around—156 sc.

Rnd 27: [2 sc in next sc, sc in next 25 sc] around—162 sc.

Rnd 28: [Sc in next 13 sc, 2 sc in next sc, sc in next 13 sc] around—168 sc.

Rnd 29: [2 sc in next sc, sc in next 27 sc] around—174 sc.

Rnd 30: [Sc in next 14 sc, 2 sc in next sc, sc in next 14 sc] around—180 sc.

Rnd 31: [2 sc in next sc, sc in next 29 sc] around—186 sc.

Rnd 32: [Sc in next 15 sc, 2 sc in next sc, sc in next 15 sc] around—192 sc.

Rnd 33: [2 sc in next sc, sc in next 31 sc] around—198 sc.

Rnd 34: [Sc in next 16 sc, 2 sc in next sc, sc in next 16 sc] around, join—204 sc.

Change to B. Begin working in joined rounds.

Rnd 35: Ch 1, [2 sc in next sc, sc in next 33 sc] around, join—210 sc.

Rnd 36: Ch 1, [sc in next 17 sc, 2 sc in next sc, sc in next 17 sc] around, join—216 sc.

Change to C.

Rnd 37: Ch 1, [2 sc in next sc, sc in next 35 sc] around, join—222 sc.

Rnd 38: Ch 1, [sc in next 18 sc, 2 sc in next sc, sc in next 18 sc] around, join—228 sc.

Rnd 39: Ch 1, [2 sc in next sc, sc in next 37 sc] around, join—234 sc.

Rnd 40: Ch 1, [sc in next 19 sc, 2 sc in next sc, sc in next 19 sc] around, join—240 sc.

Continue to Seaming.

SEAMING

With C.

Working through both thicknesses and using preferred joining method, fold circle in half and seam 30 sts on either side of fold toward opening. Leave remaining stitches unseamed for purse opening.

FINISHING

Add purse strap to either side of purse opening. Add a zipper for closing, if desired.

Using black embroidery thread, embroider small seeds on the pink part of your "Watermelon Sugar" Clutch.

"I LOVE AN ACCESSORY AS MUCH AS THE NEXT PERSON."

Harry Styles

"Cherry" Earrings

Designed by Lee Sartori

As much as "Adore You" is a song for new beginnings and the excitement of new love, "Cherry" is about the gloom and sadness of a breakup. In Harry's words, "'Cherry' is about . . . I wanted it to reflect how I felt then. I was feeling not great. It's all about being not great. Because, you get petty when things don't go the way you want it. There's parts that's so pathetic." Harry is completely relatable as he walks us through his fight with his powerful emotions of jealousy and longing after his public breakup with French model Camille Rowe. The pair dated for a year, and as Harry puts his sadness to the song, he also includes a voicemail from Rowe at the very end to emphasize his longing for the relationship they shared. In "Cherry," Harry references how there is a little bit of his lost love in the way he dresses, and I think that's so touching and endearing, as well as truthful. We take a little piece of everyone we love and hold them with us even after they are gone. The "Cherry" Earrings are a nod to the idea of carrying the good parts of the story on with us, even if it had to come to an end. These little "Cherry" Earrings are so sweet and fun to crochet. I hope you love making them!

Measurements

2" (5 cm), not including hooks

Yarn

Sock weight (#1 Super Fine)

Shown here: Lion Brand Perle 5/2 Cotton Cone Yarn, 2100 yds (1920 m), 17½ oz (499 g), 100% mercerized cotton: small amounts (less than 10g) each S157 Deep Red (A), S261 Oregano (B)

Hook

US #2 (1.5 mm) steel crochet hook.

Notions

Small amount of fiberfill

Pair of fishhook craft earrings

Scissors

Gauge

Gauge is not critical to this project.

Notes

- ♥ Earrings are worked in three parts: Cherry, Leaf, and Stem.
- ♥ Work the Cherry in continuous rounds.

Special Stitches

Inv-dec (invisible single crochet decrease): Insert hook in FLO of each of next 2 sts, yo and draw through both sts, yo and draw through 2 loops on hook—1 st decreased.

CONTINUED

CHAPTER ONE: RED CARPET

CHERRY (MAKE 4)

With A.

Rnd 1: Ch 2, 6 sc in 2nd ch from hook—6 sc.

Rnd 2: 2 sc in each sc around—12 sc.

Rnd 3: [2 sc in next sc, sc in next sc] around—18 sc.

Rnds 4–6: Sc in each sc around.

Rnd 7: [Sc in next sc, inv-dec] around—12 sc.

Stuff piece firmly.

Rnd 8: Inv-dec around—6 sc.

Fasten off, leaving a long tail for sewing. Use tail to sew remaining 6 sts closed. Weave in ends.

LEAF (MAKE 2)

With B.

Row 1: Ch 8, 2 sc in 2nd ch from hook, 2 sc in next ch, 2 hdc in next 2 ch, 2 dc in next 2 ch, 7 tr in last ch, rotate to work on underside of ch, 2 dc in next 2 ch, 2 hdc in next 2 ch, 2 sc in next 2 ch, sl st to join—31 sts.

Fasten off, weave in ends.

STEM

With B.

Row 1: Join to 1st Cherry with a sl st in any st of Rnd 8, ch 10, sl st in 4th tr of Leaf, ch 16, sl st in any st of Rnd 8 of 2nd Cherry to join.

Fasten off, weave in ends.

Rep Row 1 for 2nd Earring.

FINISHING

Secure Stem to earring hardware on the same sl st that joined the Stem to the Leaf.

"It's not like I've ever sat and done an interview and said, 'So I was in a relationship, and this is what happened'... Because, for me, music is where I let that cross over. It's the only place, strangely, where it feels right to let that cross over."

STYLE LIKE STYLES

If earrings are not your thing, these little cherries would make the perfect keychain or bag charm as well!

CHAPTER ONE: RED CARPET

Home Sweet Home
CHAPTER TWO

They say "home is where the heart is," and for this book, we think an even better fit would be "home is where my fun Harry Styles stuff is." There is nothing cozier than cuddling under some handmade blankets, and if they are an homage to Harry Styles's famous tattoos, even better! And while we're getting cozy, it's a great idea to add a "Treat People with Kindness" Pillow on one end of the couch and a *Harry's House* Pillow on the other because they look so cute! And on the table in front of you, set your tea down on your newly crocheted "Matilda" Tea and Toast Coasters, right beside your cute little sushi amigurumi from "Music for a Sushi Restaurant." And when your toes get cold, sneak your feet into your new pair of "Two Ghosts" Slippers under the table, and you're all set to go! I'm not sure if I can even picture a cozier scene than this! Happy crocheting!

"IMAGINE, IT'S A DAY IN MY HOUSE, WHAT DO I GO THROUGH? A DAY IN MY MIND, WHAT DO I GO THROUGH? IN MY HOUSE, I'M PLAYING FUN MUSIC, SAD MUSIC, I'M PLAYING THIS, I'M PLAYING THAT. IT'S A DAY IN THE LIFE."

Harry Styles

"Falling" Patchwork Pullover

Designed by Wilma Westenberg

The beautiful piano ballad "Falling" is described by Harry Styles as being about "[t]hat feeling of when you can feel yourself kind of falling back into one of those [low] moments." It's reluctantly stepping back into old habits and old ways. It's hard to go through the highs and lows in moments of instability in life, and Harry openly sings his heart out about it. Styles states that "Falling" is "[t]hat feeling of kind of being overwhelmed, you know you can feel like you're drowning sometimes . . . and the fact that it's coming from the piano, I guess it's like writing these songs are what helps but also they can hurt you sometimes." The "Falling" Patchwork Pullover is a homage to the cardigan Harry has worn on stage, a comfy, colorful patchy number that looks like the knitted version of a cozy hug. In this crochet pattern, you can explore some different textures and put together a fun version of your own! Finish off with a folded collar, and be ready to sing along with Harry next time he performs "Falling" on stage—or on the radio.

Size

XS/S/M (L/XL/2X, 3X/4X/5X)

Measurements

To fit bust: 28–38 (40–50, 52–62)" [71–96.5 (101.5–127, 132–157.5) cm]

Finished chest: 42 (54, 66)" [106.5 (137, 167.5) cm]

Finished length: 22½ (22½, 23½)" [57 (57, 59.5) cm], including lower ribbing

Yarn

Worsted weight (#4 Medium)

Shown here: Lion Brand Basic Stitch Anti-Pilling, 185 yds (170 m), 3½ oz (100 g), 100% acrylic: 3 (3, 4) balls 400G Red Heather (A), 1 (2, 2) ball(s) 133A Pumpkin (B), 1 (2, 2) ball(s) 130B Grass (C), 1 (2, 2) ball(s) 153 Black (D), 1 (2, 2) ball(s) 157X Lemonade (E), 2 (2, 2) balls 211AL Buffalo Hill (F).

Hook

US Size J/10 (6 mm) crochet hook. Adjust hook size if necessary to obtain correct gauge.

Notions

Yarn needle

Scissors

Gauge

One XS/S/M Rectangle = 3½" x 5" (9 cm x 12.5 cm)

One L/XL/2X Rectangle = 4½" x 5" (11.5 cm x 12.5 cm)

One 3X/4X/5X Rectangle = 5½" x 7" (14 cm x 18 cm)

Notes

♥ Sweater is made from 72 (72, 52) rectangles, joined together following diagrams.

♥ Rectangles and ribbings are worked separately and then joined together.

♥ The sweater has a positive ease of 4–14" (10–35.5 cm) to create an oversized fit.

♥ Turning chains do not count as stitches.

♥ To make the sweater longer or wider, create larger rectangles by adding extra rows and stitches.

♥ If using substitute yarn, ensure the rectangle measurements are correct and adjust the stitches and rows accordingly.

CONTINUED

CHAPTER TWO: HOME SWEET HOME

RECTANGLE A: HDC RIB (MAKE 12 [12, 8])

With A.

Row 1: Ch 20 (20, 27), hdc in 3rd ch from hook and in each ch across, turn—18 (18, 25) hdc.

Rows 2–7 (9, 11): Ch 2 (does not count as a st here and throughout), hdc BLO in each st across, turn.

Fasten off.

RECTANGLE B: CH-1 MESH (MAKE 12 [12, 8])

With B.

Row 1: Ch 14 (18, 22), sc in 2nd ch from hook, [ch 1, skip next ch, sc in next ch] across, turn—7 (9, 11) sc, 6 (8, 10) ch-1 spaces.

Rows 2–18 (18, 25): Ch 1, sc in first sc, [ch 1, skip next ch-1 space, sc in next sc] across, turn.

Fasten off.

RECTANGLE C: SC RIB (MAKE 12 [12, 10])

With C.

Row 1: Ch 18 (18, 25), sc in 2nd ch from hook and in each ch across, turn—17 (17, 24) sc.

Rows 2–13 (17, 20): Ch 1, sc BLO in each st across, turn.

Fasten off.

RECTANGLE D: SC/DC ROWS (MAKE 12 [12, 9])

With D.

Row 1: Ch 17 (17, 23), sc in 2nd ch from hook and in each ch across, turn—16 (16, 17) sts.

Row 2: Ch 3, dc in each st across, turn.

Row 3: Ch 1, sc in each st across, turn.

Rows 4–9 (11, 14): Rep Rows 2 and 3.

Fasten off.

RECTANGLE E: DC/SC STITCHES (MAKE 12 [12, 8])

With E.

Row 1: Ch 13 (17, 19), dc in 4th ch from hook, [sc in next ch, dc in next ch] across to last ch, sc in last ch, turn—10 (14, 16) sts.

Rows 2–11 (11, 15): Ch 3, [dc in next sc, sc in next dc] across, turn.

Fasten off.

RECTANGLE F: SOLID DC (MAKE 12 [12, 9])

With F.

Row 1: Ch 13 (16, 19), dc in 4th ch from hook and in each ch across, turn—10 (13, 16) dc.

Rows 2–9 (9, 13): Ch 3, dc across, turn.

Fasten off.

"I DIDN'T WANT TO WRITE STORIES. I WANTED TO WRITE MY STORIES, THINGS THAT HAPPENED TO ME. THE NUMBER ONE THING WAS, I WANTED TO BE HONEST. I HADN'T DONE THAT BEFORE."

CHAPTER TWO: HOME SWEET HOME

LAYOUT DIAGRAMS

Size 3X/4X/5X
FRONT

E	F		B	C	F	A	E	D		B	A
C	D									C	D
			E	D	A	B	C	F			
			F	B	C	D	A	E			

BACK

D	C		D	A	C	F	E	B		A	C
F	B									F	E
			B	D	F	E	A	C			
			C	E	A	D	B	F			

KEY

Rectangle A:
Hdc Rib worked with Red Heather

Rectangle B:
Ch-1 Mesh worked with Pumpkin

Rectangle C:
Sc Rib worked with Grass

Rectangle D:
Sc/Dc Rows worked with Black

Rectangle E:
Dc/Sc Stitches worked with Lemonade

Rectangle F:
Solid DC worked with Buffalo Hill

Sizes XS/S/M and L/XL/2X
FRONT

B	E	F		B	C	F	A	E	D		B	A	E
A	C	D									C	D	F
				E	D	A	B	C	F				
				F	B	C	D	A	E				
				A	E	B	F	D	C				

BACK

A	D	C		D	A	C	F	E	B		A	C	D
E	F	B									F	E	B
				B	D	F	E	A	C				
				C	E	A	D	B	F				
				E	F	B	C	A	D				

RECTANGLE ASSEMBLY

Sl st the rectangles together as shown in the diagrams. You can also use a tapestry needle to sew the rectangles together.

Tip: Use red yarn as much as possible and join other colored rectangles with leftover yarn.

With RS facing each other, lay the front panel on top of the back panel. Sl st or sew the sides together, starting at the bottom and continuing to the armpit and sleeve. Sl st or sew the shoulders together for 2 rectangles, or 7 (9, 11)" (18 (23, 28) cm). Weave in all ends, and turn the work inside out.

RIBBING FOR BOTTOM

With A.

Row 1: Ch 12, hdc in 3rd ch and in each ch across, turn—10 hdc.

Rows 2–84 (108, 132): Ch 2, hdc BLO in each st across, turn.

Note: Ribbing should measure 42 (54, 66)" (106.5 (137, 167.5) cm).

Sl st short ends together; insert hook in the BLO of the st and ch. Turn ribbing inside out. Sl st or sew ribbing along bottom of sweater.

STYLE LIKE STYLES

Make an extra patch and sew it on the front panel to add a front pocket to this amazing pullover!

CHAPTER TWO: HOME SWEET HOME

CONTINUED

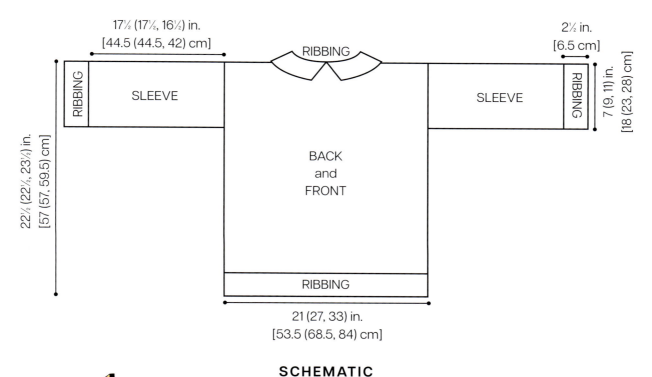

SCHEMATIC

RIBBING FOR CUFFS (MAKE 2)

With A.

Row 1: Ch 12 (12, 16), hdc in 3rd ch and in each ch across, turn—10 (10, 14) hdc.

Rows 2–26 (34, 42): Ch 2, hdc BLO in each st across, turn.

Note: Ribbing should measure 13 (17, 21)" (33 (43, 53.5 cm).

Sl st short ends together; insert hook in the BLO of the st and ch. Turn ribbing inside out. Sl st or sew the ribbings to the sleeves.

Tip: If you prefer narrower cuffs, you can make them smaller by reducing the number of rows.

RIBBING FOR NECKLINE

With A.

Row 1: Ch 12, hdc in 3rd ch and in each ch across, turn—10 hdc.

Rows 2–41 (53, 65): Ch 2, hdc BLO in each st across, turn.

Note: Ribbing should measure 20 (26, 32)" (51 (66, 81.5) cm).

Sew or sl st the ribbing to the neckline, beginning and ending at center front of neck.

Weave in all ends.

CHAPTER TWO: HOME SWEET HOME

STYLE LIKE STYLES

Change the color of the beaded border to match your favorite chunky beaded necklace!

Harry's House Pillow

Designed by Lee Sartori

Welcome home! There is nothing better than opening the front door of your place and feeling the weight of the world melt from your shoulders. It's where you can relax and just be yourself. It's where you can dream about the future and plan for the day. In *Harry's House*, Harry Styles set out to explore the inner workings of his mind and what it's like to live there. The album is an introspective collection of fantastic songs filled with hopes and dreams and a huge amount of charm. The *Harry's House* Pillow is a project inspired by Harry's release of the album in 2022 and the 40-second trailer featuring the facade of a house that rises near him. Harry can also be seen wearing an adorable *Harry's House* jumper with a cute little house drawing while promoting the new album. This pillow is a fun nod to that jumper and to the green chunky necklace that Harry wears. You will start this crochet pattern with the pillow panels and finish with the fun beaded border at the end. Add the pillow to your favorite crochet spot, and get extra cozy and cuddly!

Measurements

20" x 20" (51 cm x 51 cm) with beaded border

Yarn

Worsted weight (#4 Medium)

Shown here: Lion Brand Pound of Love, 1,020 yds (932 m), 16 oz (454 g), 100% acrylic: 1 ball 156A Pastel Green (A)

Shown here: Lion Brand Vanna's Choice, 170 yds (156 m), 3½ oz (100 g), 100% acrylic: 1 ball each 113 Scarlet (B), 172C Kelly Green (C)

Hooks

US Size H/8 (5 mm) crochet hook. Adjust hook size if necessary to obtain correct gauge.

US size G/6 (4 mm) crochet hook.

Notions

18" x 18" (45.5 cm x 45.5 cm) pillow form

Fiberfill

Yarn needle

Scissors

Gauge

18 sc x 18 rows = 4" (10 cm), with larger crochet hook

Notes

♥ Front Panel of Pillow uses a color chart to create the image.

♥ Change colors by drawing new color through last yarn over of previous stitch.

♥ Carry color not in use along back of panel, stitch over the top of the carried strand every 5 stitches to avoid long floats.

Special Stitches

Inv-dec (invisible single crochet decrease): Insert hook in FLO of each of next 2 sts, yo and draw through both sts, yo and draw through 2 loops on hook—1 st decreased.

CONTINUED

BACK PANEL

With A and larger crochet hook.

Row 1: Ch 69, sc in 2nd ch from hook and in each ch across, turn—68 sc.

Rows 2–68: Ch 1, sc across, turn.

FRONT PANEL

With A and B and larger crochet hook, work same as Back Panel AND change yarn color following House chart. Fasten off.

BORDER

Hold Front and Back Panels with WS together, with sts and ends of rows matching, and Front Panel on top.

Rnd 1: Draw up a loop of A in top left corner to work in ends of rows along side edge, ch 1, work sc in end of each of 68 rows along side edge, ch 1, sc in each of next 68 ch along bottom edge, ch 1, sc in end of each of 68 rows along next side edge, insert pillow form, ch 1, sc in each st of Row 68, ch 1, join—272 sc, 4 ch-1 spaces.

Rnd 2: Ch 2 (does not count as a st here and throughout) [hdc in each sc to next ch-1 space, ch 1, skip ch-1 space] 4 times, join—272 hdc, 4 ch-1 spaces.

Rnds 3 and 4: Ch 2, [hdc in BLO of each hdc to next ch-1 space, ch 1, skip ch-1 space] 4 times, join.

Fasten off, weave in ends.

BEADS (MAKE 32)

With C and smaller crochet hook.

Rnd 1: Ch 2, 6 sc in 2nd ch from hook—6 sc.

Rnd 2: 2 sc in each sc around—12 sc.

Rnds 3 and 4: Sc in each sc around.

Rnd 5: Inv-dec around—6 sc.

Fasten off, leaving a long tail for sewing. Stuff Bead. Use tail to sew remaining 6 sts closed. Weave in ends.

BEADED BORDER

With C and smaller hook.

Rnd 1: Sl st to any corner ch-1 space, ch 1, *sc in next 2 sts, [sc in next 2 sts, sl st to top of a Bead, ch 6, sl st in bottom of same Bead, skip next 4 sts on Pillow, sc in next 2 sts] 8 times, sc in next 2 sts, skip next ch-1 space; rep from * around, join—32 Beads, 32 ch-6, 144 sc.

Fasten off, weave in ends.

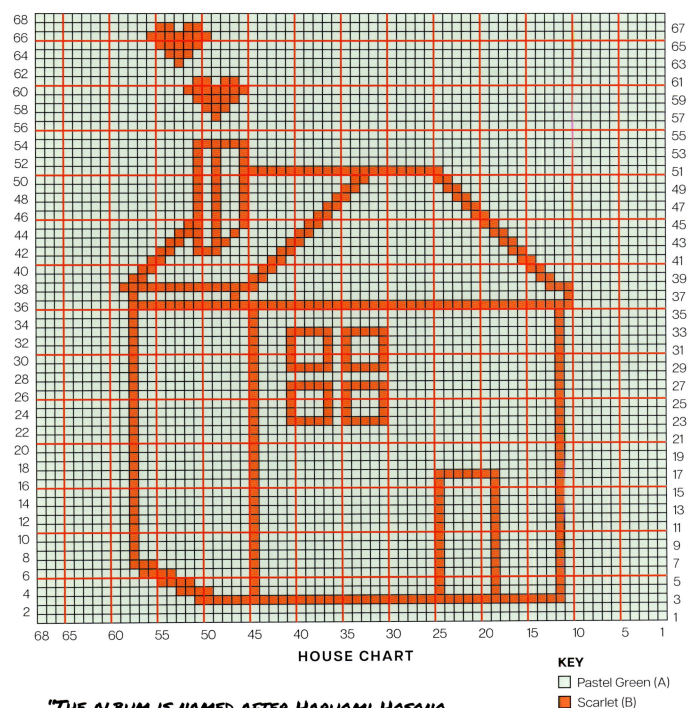

"THE ALBUM IS NAMED AFTER HARUOMI HOSONO, HE HAD AN ALBUM IN THE '70S CALLED HOSONO'S HOUSE [SIC], AND I SPENT THAT CHUNK IN JAPAN AND HEARD THAT RECORD, AND I WAS LIKE, 'I LOVE THAT... IT'D BE REALLY FUN TO MAKE A RECORD CALLED HARRY'S HOUSE.'"

— Harry Styles

CHAPTER TWO: HOME SWEET HOME

Skill Level 1

"Music for a Sushi Restaurant" Sushi

Designed by Lee Sartori

Have you ever been sitting down at your favorite restaurant, enjoying some delicious food, when all of a sudden you clue into the music playing? I used to go to a Thai food restaurant that played what we referred to as "elevator music" of hit movie soundtracks, and when the song for *Titanic* would come on, we would all look at each other like, "What is happening?" It can be so funny, and if you go often enough, it becomes part of the charm! In "Music for a Sushi Restaurant," Harry Styles wanted to capture that feeling of sitting in a restaurant and cluing in to the music playing that doesn't seem to match the vibe. It can be a good thing or a bad thing depending on the mood of the place and depending on the music choice! But if I were sitting in a sushi restaurant and Harry's song came on, I would be dancing in my seat for sure. It's such a joyful beat and a happy vibe. To celebrate this exuberant expression of love for the music in a sushi restaurant, I created four little amigurumi sushi for you to crochet and keep with you. They are small but mighty, just like how a sushi roll with a bit of wasabi can pack a punch!

Measurements

2½" x 1" (6.5 cm x 2.5 cm)

Yarn

Worsted weight (#4 Medium)

Shown here: Lion Brand Basic Stitch Anti-Pilling, 185 yds (170 m), 3½ oz (100 g), 100% acrylic: 1 ball each 100 White (A), 133A Pumpkin (B), 184S Peachy (C), 157X Lemonade (D), 153 Black (E), 173A Sage (F)

Hook

US Size C/2 (2.5 mm) crochet hook. Adjust hook size if necessary to obtain correct gauge.

Notions

4 pairs of 6 mm black safety eyes

Small amount of fiberfill

Black embroidery thread

Yarn needle

Scissors

Stitch marker

Gauge

Gauge is not critical to this project.

22 sc x 24 rows = 4" (10 cm)

Notes

♥ Sushi body is worked in continuous rounds unless otherwise indicated; use a stitch marker to track rounds.

♥ When using 2 colors, drop unused color and pick it up when needed. Do not carry it under working stitches.

♥ Ch 1 does not count as a stitch.

♥ Join by slip stitching in 1st stitch.

Special Stitches

Inv-dec (invisible single crochet decrease): Insert hook in FLO of each of next 2 sc, yo and draw through both sc, yo and draw through 2 loops on hook—1 st decreased.

CONTINUED

CHAPTER TWO: HOME SWEET HOME

73

RICE BALL (MAKE 3)

With A.

Rnd 1: Ch 6, sc in 2nd ch from hook, sc in next 3 ch, 3 sc in last ch, rotate to work on underside of starting ch, sc in next 4 ch, 3 sc in last ch (this is the ch that was skipped at the beg of this rnd)—14 sc.

Rnd 2: [Sc in next 4 sc, 2 sc in next 3 sc] twice—20 sc.

Rnd 3: *Sc in next 4 sc, [2 sc in next sc, sc in next sc] 3 times; rep from * around—26 sc.

Rnd 4: Working in BLO, sc in each sc around.

Add safety eyes between Rnds 1 and 2 in center of increases. With embroidery thread, embroider a small mouth one round below eyes.

Rnds 5–16: Sc in each sc around.

Rnd 17: Working in BLO, sc in each sc around.

Rnd 18: Inv-dec, sc in next 4 sc, [sc in next sc, inv-dec] 3 times, sc in next 4 sc, sc in next sc, [inv-dec, sc in next sc] twice—20 sc.

Stuff rice ball.

Rnd 19: Inv-dec, sc in next 4 sc, [inv-dec] 3 times, sc in next 4 sc, [inv-dec] twice—14 sc.

Fasten off, leaving a long tail for sewing. Sew remaining stitches closed, matching 7 stitches on either side (longways). Weave in ends.

SUSHI #1: FISH NIGIRI

With B and alternating between B and A each round.

Rnd 1: Ch 2, 6 sc in 2nd ch from hook, join—6 sc.

Rnd 2: Ch 1, 2 sc in each sc, join—12 sc.

Rnd 3: Ch 1, *2 sc in next sc, sc in next sc; rep from * around, join—18 sc.

Rnds 4–13: Ch 1, sc in each sc around, join.

Rnd 14: Ch 1, *sc in next sc, inv-dec; rep from * around, join—12 sc.

Rnd 15: Ch 1, inv-dec around, join—6 sc.

Fasten off A, continue with B only. Begin working in turned rows for tail.

Row 16: Ch 7, sc in 2nd ch from hook, sc in next 5 ch, sl st in next sc of Rnd 15, turn—6 sc.

Row 17: Ch 1, working in BLO, sc in next 4 sc, turn leaving remaining sc unworked—4 sc.

Row 18: Ch 1, working in BLO, [sc2tog] twice, sl st in next sc of Rnd 15, turn—2 sc.

Row 19: Ch 1, working in BLO, 2 sc in next 2 sc, turn—4 sc.

Row 20: Ch 1, 2 sc in each of next 2 sc, sc in next 2 sc, sl st in next sc of Rnd 15—6 sc.

Fasten off, weave in ends.

Sew Sushi #1 to the top of the Rice Ball. Weave in ends.

SUSHI #1

SUSHI #2

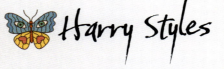

"I WAS IN A SUSHI RESTAURANT IN LOS ANGELES WITH MY PRODUCER AND ONE OF OUR SONGS CAME ON FROM THE LAST ALBUM, AND I KIND OF SAID LIKE, THIS IS REALLY STRANGE. AND THEN I WAS LIKE, OH, THAT WOULD BE A REALLY FUN ALBUM TITLE. AND THEN AS THIS, AS THIS—AS THE SONGS STARTED BEING MADE, I KIND OF JUST SAID 'MUSIC FOR A SUSHI RESTAURANT.'"

Harry Styles

CHAPTER TWO: HOME SWEET HOME

STYLE LIKE STYLES

These little sushi would be so cute on a little dish on a coffee table, or hung from a mobile in a baby's room! The possibilities are endless.

UNOFFICIAL HARRY STYLES CROCHET

SUSHI #2: TAI NIGIRI

With C.

Row 1: Ch 13, sc in 2nd ch from hook, sc in each ch across, turn—12 sc.

Rows 2–10: Ch 1, sc across, turn.

Fasten off, leaving a long tail for sewing. Sew Sushi #2 to the top of a Rice Ball. Weave in ends.

SUSHI #3: TAMAGO NIGIRI

With D.

Rnds 1–15: With D only, rep Rnds 1–15 of Sushi #1.

Fasten off, leaving a long tail for sewing. Sew to the top of last Rice Ball; weave in ends. Continue to Seaweed Wrap.

SEAWEED WRAP

With E.

Rnd 1: Ch 30, join to form a ring, ch 1, sc in each ch around, join—30 sc.

Fasten off, leaving a tail for sewing. Wrap Seaweed around entire Sushi #3, and secure with yarn tail. Weave in ends.

SUSHI #4: FUTO URA MAKI ROLL

With B.

Rnd 1: Ch 2, 2 sc in 2nd ch from hook with B, 2 sc in same ch with F, 2 sc in same ch with D, join—6 sc.

Rnd 2: Ch 1, 2 sc in next 2 sc with B, 2 sc in next 2 sc with F, 2 sc in next 2 sc with D, join—12 sc.

Rnd 3: Ch 1, [2 sc in next sc, sc in next sc] twice with B, [2 sc in next sc, sc in next sc] twice with F, [2 sc in next sc, sc in next sc] twice with D, join—18 sc.

Change to E.

Rnd 4: Ch 1, [2 sc in next sc, sc in next 2 sc] around, join—24 sc.

Change to A.

Rnd 5: Ch 1, [2 sc in next sc, sc in next 3 sc] around, join—30 sc.

Rnd 6: Ch 1, [sc in next 2 sc, 2 sc in next sc, sc in next 2 sc] around, join—36 sc.

Rnd 7: Ch 1, working in BLO, sc in each sc around, join.

Rnds 8–12: Ch 1, sc in each sc around, join.

Fasten off. Add safety eyes between Rnds 10 and 11. Add smile to Rnd 12 using black embroidery thread.

BOTTOM

Rnds 1–6: Rep Rnds 1–6 of Sushi #4.

Fasten off, leaving a long tail for sewing. Stuff Sushi #4. Sew Bottom to Rnd 12. Weave in ends.

SUSHI #3

SUSHI #4

CHAPTER TWO: HOME SWEET HOME

"Matilda" Tea and Toast Coasters

Designed by Lee Sartori

What I loved the most about growing up was the ability and agency to choose my family and surround myself with support and love. I am lucky enough to have friends in my life that I consider my soulmates, people who show up and provide the constant and consistent care everyone needs as they go through life. If the song "Matilda" resonates with you on a deep level like it does with me, I wish I could give you a hug! One of the reasons I love this song so much is that it is so warm and forgiving. And to me, it's just the right amount of sad too. It invites you to enjoy the sunshine on dark days. It invites you to throw a party. It reminds you that you have agency in your decisions and can and should choose what is best for you without guilt. So, pull up a comfy chair. You're just in time for some tea and toast and a friendly face. The "Matilda" Tea and Toast Coasters nod to the gentle and endearing song featured on the *Harry's House* album. These coasters are worked in cotton yarn to protect them from the hot mugs set down on them. Make as many as you need for settings at your table, and invite your friends to join you in whatever joy you are celebrating today.

Measurements

Tea coasters: 5" x 4" (12.5 cm x 10 cm) each

Toast coasters: 4.5" x 4" (11.5 cm x 10 cm) each

Yarn

Worsted weight (#4 Medium)

Shown here: Lion Brand 24/7 Cotton 186 yds (170 m), 3½ oz (100 g), 100% mercerized cotton: 1 ball each 107I Sky (A), 124A Camel (B), 144L Magenta (C), 098C Ecru (D), 157D Lemon (E), 126AA Café Au Lait (F)

Hook

US Size C/2 (2.5 mm) crochet hook. Adjust hook size if necessary to obtain correct gauge.

Notions

Black embroidery thread

Pink blush

Yarn needle

Scissors

Stitch marker

Gauge

Gauge is not critical to this project.

24 sc x 26 rows = 4" (10 cm)

Notes

♥ Ch 1 does not count as a stitch.

♥ Ch 2 counts as a double crochet.

STYLE LIKE STYLES
Change the butter or jam colors to match your favorite spread for your toast!

CHAPTER TWO: HOME SWEET HOME

CUP (MAKE 1 WITH A AND 1 WITH C)

With A for 1st Cup and C for 2nd Cup.

Row 1: Ch 2, 3 sc in 2nd ch from hook, turn—3 sc.

Row 2: Ch 1, 2 sc in each sc, turn—6 sc.

Row 3: Ch 1, [2 sc in next sc, sc in next sc] across, turn—9 sc.

Row 4: Ch 1, [2 sc in next sc, sc in next 2 sc] across, turn—12 sc.

Row 5: Ch 1, [2 sc in next sc, sc in next 3 sc] across, turn—15 sc.

Row 6: Ch 1, [2 sc in next sc, sc in next 4 sc] across, turn—18 sc.

Row 7: Ch 1, [2 sc in next sc, sc in next 5 sc] across, turn—21 sc.

Row 8: Ch 1, [2 sc in next sc, sc in next 6 sc] across, turn—24 sc.

Row 9: Ch 1, [2 sc in next sc, sc in next 7 sc] across, turn—27 sc.

Row 10: Ch 1, [2 sc in next sc, sc in next 8 sc] across, turn—30 sc.

Row 11: Rotate to work across row ends, do not ch 1, work 20 sc evenly across row ends, turn—20 sc.

Rows 12–16: Ch 1, sc in each sc across, turn.

Rows 17 and 18: Ch 2, dc in next 2 sc, hdc in next 3 sc, sc in next 8 sc, hdc in next 3 sc, dc in last 3 sc—20 sts.

Change to B.

Rows 19 and 20: Ch 1, sc in next 3 sts, hdc in next 3 sts, dc in next 8 sts, hdc in next 3 sts, sc in next 3 sts, turn.

Change back to A for 1st Cup, and C for 2nd Cup.

Row 21 (border): Ch 1, sc in each st across, rotate to work in row ends, do not ch 1, work 11 sc evenly across row ends, [2 sc in next st, sc in next 9 sts] 3 times across Row 10 sts, work 11 sc evenly across row ends, sl st to join—75 sc.

Fasten off, weave in ends, and continue to Cup Handle.

CUP HANDLE (MAKE 1 WITH A AND 1 WITH C)

With A for 1st Cup and C for 2nd Cup.

Leave a long tail at beg for sewing.

Row 1: Ch 21, starting in 2nd ch from hook, sc in back bump of each ch across, turn—20 sc.

Row 2: Ch 1, sl st in each sc across—20 sl st.

Fasten off, leaving a long tail for sewing. Sew Cup Handle to right side of Cup between Rows 11 and 19. Weave in ends.

UNOFFICIAL HARRY STYLES CROCHET

TOAST WITH JAM

With D.

Row 1: Ch 21, sc in 2nd ch from hook and in each ch across, turn—20 sc.

Rows 2–14: Ch 1, sc in each sc across, turn.

Row 15: Ch 1, sc in next 6 sc with D, sc in next sc with C, sc in next 13 with D, turn.

Row 16: Ch 1, 2 sc in next sc with D, sc in next 11 sc with D, sc in next 3 sc with C, sc in next 4 sc with D, 2 sc in next sc with D, turn—22 sc.

Row 17: Ch 1, 2 sc in next sc with D, sc in next 3 sc with D, sc in next 5 sc with C, sc in next 12 sc with D, 2 sc in last sc with D, turn—24 sc.

Row 18: Ch 1, 2 sc in next sc with D, sc in next 12 sc with D, sc in next 6 sc with C, sc in next 4 sc with D, 2 sc in last sc with D, turn—26 sc.

Row 19: Ch 1, sc in next 6 sc with D, sc in next 6 sc with C, sc in next 14 sc with D, turn.

Row 20: Ch 1, sc in next 15 sc with D, sc in next 5 sc with C, sc in next 6 sc with D, turn.

Row 21: Ch 1, sc2tog with D, sc in next 4 sc with D, sc in next 4 sc with C, sc in next 14 sc with D, sc2tog with D, turn—24 sc.

Row 22: Ch 1, sc2tog with D, sc in next 14 sc with D, sc in next 2 sc with C, sc in next 4 sc with D, sc2tog with D, turn—22 sc.

Fasten off C, continue with D.

Row 23: Ch 1, sc in next sc, hdc in next 3 sc, dc in next 3 sc, hdc in next 2 sc, sc in next 4 sc, hdc in next 2 sc, dc in next 3 sc, hdc in next 3 sc, sc in last sc, turn.

Rnd 24 (border): Rotate to work in row ends, do not ch 1, work 22 sc evenly down side, 3 sc in corner, sc in next 20 ch along bottom edge, rotate to crochet up next side, 3 sc in 1st row end, work 22 sc evenly up side, 2 sc in 1st st of Row 23, sc next 21 sts, join—93 sc.

Change to F.

Rnd 25: Ch 1, sc in next 23 sc, 3 sc in corner, sc in next 22 sc, 3 sc in corner, sc in next 23 sc, 2 sc in corner, sc in next 21 sc, 2 sc in last sc, join—99 sc.

Fasten off; weave in ends.

"I WANT TO GIVE YOU SOMETHING, I WANT TO SUPPORT YOU IN SOME WAY, BUT IT'S NOT NECESSARILY MY PLACE TO MAKE IT ABOUT ME BECAUSE IT'S NOT MY EXPERIENCE. SOMETIMES IT'S JUST ABOUT LISTENING. I HOPE THAT'S WHAT I DID HERE. IF NOTHING ELSE, IT JUST SAYS, 'I WAS LISTENING TO YOU.'" —Harry Styles

TOAST WITH BUTTER

Rep all instructions for Toast with Jam, changing C for E in Rows 15–22.

FINISHING

Using black embroidery thread, add eyes to Cups between Rows 3 and 4 and mouth between Rows 5 and 6. Add a small amount of blush to cheeks under eyes.

Using black embroidery thread, add eyes to Toast between Rows 8 and 9 and mouth between Rows 10 and 11. Add a small amount of blush to cheeks under eyes.

CHAPTER TWO: HOME SWEET HOME

"Two Ghosts" Slippers

Designed by Julie Desjardins

It can be so difficult to say goodbye in love, but even before then, it can be even more heartbreaking when you recognize the exact moment that something is broken and can't be fixed. It kicks in all of a sudden, and you find yourself mourning the loss before it even happens. It feels like becoming a ghost of your former self going through the motions of a life you know you can't continue living. "Two Ghosts" is about being stuck in that moment of realization, the mournful process of coming to terms with the idea that the relationship that used to make you so happy just wasn't meant to last. The song is a forlorn bid to reclaim a person's own humanity after a relationship ends. The "Two Ghosts" Slippers are a nod to the ghosts Harry Styles sings about as they search around for a heartbeat. Although the song is ultimately a sad one, these slippers bring a bit of comfort and warmth. They remind me of the time after a breakup when you get all cozy, wrap yourself in a blanket, and eat an entire tub of ice cream. So, don't forget to wear your cute ghostly "slippy slips" and treat yourself. I hope they bring you comfort and joy!

Size

S (M, L, XL)

Measurements

To fit US shoe sizes: Youth 4–6/Women's 4–6½ (Women's 7–9½/Men's 6–8½, Women's 10–12½/Men's 9–11½, Men's 10–12½)

Finished foot length: 8½ (9¾, 10¾, 11¾)" [21.5 (25, 27.5, 30) cm]

Yarn

Bulky weight (#5 Chunky)

Shown here: Lion Brand Feels Like Bliss, 109 yds (100 m), 3½ oz (100 g), 100% nylon: 2 balls 151H Sterling (A), 2 balls 150N Slate (B), small quantity 134AB Peach (C)

Hook

US Size L/11 (8 mm) crochet hook. Adjust hook size if necessary to obtain correct gauge.

US Size K/10½ (6.5 mm) crochet hook.

Notions

Yarn needle

Stitch marker

Scissors

Black felt (for eyes and mouth)

Fabric glue

Pink embroidery thread (for cheeks)

Sewing needle

Sole inserts (optional)

Gauge

11 sc x 8 rounds = 4" (10 cm), using larger hook

Notes

- ♥ Crochet 2 Half-Soles for each slipper (a total of 4) in the round and assemble them in pairs. For additional comfort and durability, add sole inserts between the Half-Soles before you finish assembling them.
- ♥ The Ghosts, or tops of the slippers, are crocheted separately in rows and sewn to the Soles. Each sole and size has a slightly different bottom.
- ♥ A Tiny Heart is crocheted in the round to decorate one of the slippers.
- ♥ Features are cut from felt or embroidered as the last step.

CHAPTER TWO: HOME SWEET HOME

HALF-SOLE (MAKE 4)

With larger hook and 2 strands of B held together.

Rnd 1 (RS): Ch 13 (16, 20, 22), sc in 2nd ch from hook and in each ch across, do not turn; working along opposite side of foundation chain, sc in each ch across, do not join or turn in this section, work in continuous rnds (spiral)—24 (30, 38, 42) sc.

Place a marker in last sc made to indicate end of rnd. Move marker up as each rnd is completed.

Rnd 2: Ch 1, 2 sc in next st, sc in next 5 (6, 8, 9) sts, hdc in next 5 (7, 9, 10) sts, 2 hdc in each of next 2 sts, hdc in next 5 (7, 9, 10) sts, sc in next 5 (6, 8, 9) sts, 2 sc in last st—28 (34, 42, 46) sts.

Rnd 3: Ch 1, 2 sc in each of next 2 sts, sc in next 5 (6, 8, 9) sts, hdc in next 5 (7, 9, 10) sts, 2 hdc in each of next 4 sts, hdc in next 5 (7, 9, 10) sts, sc in next 5 (6, 8, 9) sts, 2 sc in each last 2 sts—36, (42, 50, 54) sts.

Size S and M end here.

Sizes L and XL only:

Rnd 4: Ch 1, 2 sc in next st, sc in next st, 2 sc in next st, sc in next 9 (10) sts, hdc in next 10 (11) sts, 2 hdc in next st, hdc in next st, 2 hdc in next 2 sts, hdc in next st, 2 hdc in next st, hdc in next 10 (11) sts, sc in next 9 (10) sts, 2 sc in next st, sc in next st, 2 sc in last st—58 (62) sts.

Size L end here.

Size XL only:

Rnd 5: Ch 1, 2 sc in next st, sc in next 29 sts, 2 sc in next 2 sts, sc in next 29 sts, 2 sc in last st—66 sc.

Fasten off and weave ends in.

SOLE

Holding 2 Half-Soles together, join 2 strands of B with sl st to work through both thicknesses.

Rnd 1: Ch 1, sc in each st around, join with sl st in first sc—36 (42, 58, 66) sc.

Optional: Before finishing assembly, place a sole insert inside the slipper Sole.

Rnd 2: Ch 1, sc BLO in each st around, join with sl st in first sc.

Fasten off, and weave ends in.

Rep for second Slipper, but TURN before Rnd 2.

STYLE LIKE STYLES

These slippers are so comfy, but for added protection feel free to add nonskid bottoms to them for extra grip around the house.

UNOFFICIAL HARRY STYLES CROCHET

GHOST (TOP OF THE SLIPPER, MAKE 2)

With larger hook and 2 strands of A held together.

Row 1 (WS): Ch 10 (12, 14, 16) sc in 2nd ch from hook and in each ch across, turn—9 (11, 13, 15) sc.

Rows 2–6 (7, 8, 9): Ch 1, sc in each st across, turn.

Next 3 (4, 5, 6) rows: Ch 1, skip first st, sc in each st across to last 2 sts, skip next st, sc in last st, turn—3 sts remain in last row. At the end of the last row, do not turn.

Rnd 1: Sc in each row end toward foundation ch, across starting chs work Ghost Bottom for your size below, sc in each row end toward last row, sc in last 3 sts; join with sl st in first sc.

Fasten off and weave ends in.

Ghost Bottom (Left Slipper)

S: Hdc in next st, dc in next st, sl st in next st, hdc in next st, dc in next st, hdc in next st, sl st in next st, dc in next st, hdc in next st.

M: [Hdc in next st, dc in next st, hdc in next st, sl st in next st] twice, hdc in next st, dc in next st, hdc in last st.

L: Sl st in next st, [hdc in next st, dc in next st, hdc in next st, sl st in next st] 3 times.

XL: Sl st in next st, hdc in next st, [hdc in next st, dc in next st, hdc in next st, sl st in next st] twice, hdc in next st, dc in next st, hdc in next 2 sts, sl st in last st.

Ghost Bottom (Right Slipper)

S: Sc in next st, hdc in next st, dc in next st, hdc in next st, sl st in next st, hdc in next st, dc in next st, hdc in next st, sc in last st.

M: Sc in next st, hdc in next st, dc in next st, hdc in next st, sc in next st, sl st in next st, sc in next st, hdc in next st, dc in next st, hdc in next st, sc in last st.

L: Sc in next st, hdc in next st, dc in next 2 sts, hdc in next st, sc in next st, sl st in next st, sc in next st, hdc in next st, dc in next 2 sts, hdc in next st, sc in last st.

XL: Sc in next st, hdc in next 2 sts, dc in next 2 sts, hdc in next st, sc in next st, sl st in next st, sc in next st, hdc in next st, dc in next 2 sts, hdc in next 2 sts, sc in last st.

CONTINUED

ASSEMBLY

Position last row of Ghost on top of the hdc end of an assembled Sole. Pin in place. Ghost covers approximately half the length of the Sole.

Join 2 strands of A with a sl st to work through both thicknesses. Sew Rnd 1 of Ghost to Rnd 2 of Sole. Fasten off, and weave ends in.

Rep for second Slipper.

TINY HEART

With smaller hook and one strand of C.

Rnd 1 (RS): Leaving a long tail, ch 2, 6 sc in 2nd ch from hook, sl st in first sc to join, do not turn; work in continuous rnd (spiral)—6 sc.

Rnd 2: Skip next st, (dc, tr, dc) in next st, dc in next st, (dr, tr) in next st, dc in next st, (dc, tr, dc) in last st; join sl st in center of Heart.

Fasten off, leaving a long tail for assembly.

FINISHING

Using templates and black felt, cut out the features. Glue to Slippers as pictured. With black embroidery thread and using the photo as a guide, stitch around the perimeter of each felt piece using a running stitch. Fasten off and weave in ends.

Eyes: approx 1–1¼" (25–31 mm) height x ⁸⁄₁₀" (20 mm) width

Mouth: ¾" (19 mm) diameter

Cheeks: approx ¾–1" (19–25 mm) length

Eyes: approx 1–1¼" (25–31 mm) height x ⁸⁄₁₀" (20 mm) width

Mouth: ⁸⁄₁₀" (20 mm) height x ¾" (19 mm) width

Cheeks: approx ¾–1" (19–25 mm) length

With pink thread, embroider the cheeks.

Using long tails, attach Tiny Heart to the Slipper of your choice.

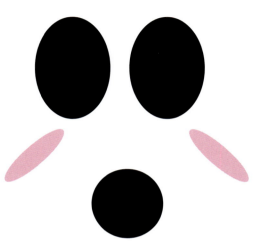

LEFT SLIPPER TEMPLATE

RIGHT SLIPPER TEMPLATE

Scan to access downloadable templates.

"AGES AGO, MY GIRLFRIEND HAD THIS LITTLE PARK NEAR HER HOUSE, WITH A BRIDGE RUNNING OVER A STREAM, AND I SET UP ALL THESE CANDLES ON THE BRIDGE. BUT WHEN I CALLED HER AND TOLD HER, SHE SAID IT WAS TOO DARK AND SHE WASN'T COMING OUT."

CHAPTER TWO: HOME SWEET HOME

"Treat People with Kindness" Pillow

Designed by Lee Sartori

In 2017, Harry Styles wore a new badge on his guitar strap during a concert for his self-titled debut album, sparking intense interest amongst his fans and ultimately leading to "Treat People with Kindness" (TPWK) becoming his self-proclaimed mantra. "TPWK" is an upbeat and jolly song filled with good vibes and an inclusive message. It offers a sense of belonging, happiness, and joy and comes with a nod to the vocal stylings of David Bowie. "I'd seen this clip of David Bowie talking, saying that you usually end up doing your best work when you feel like you can't quite touch the bottom, and realizing that the fact that it made me feel a little uncomfortable didn't mean it was a bad song was a big thing," Harry explains in an interview with *Music Week*. The TPWK Pillow is a retro flower that nods to the "flower power" movement of the '60s. Made with chunky yarn, this pillow adds the perfect touch to your cozy space. Make them in contrasting colors to add a pop of brightness to your favorite crochet spot!

Measurements

18" x 20" (45.5 cm x 51 cm)

Yarn

Super Bulky weight (#6 Super Bulky)

Shown here: Lion Brand Hometown Bonus Bundle, 162 yds (148 m), 10 oz (284 g), 100% acrylic: 1 ball 159K Madison Mustard (A), 2 balls 101AE Providence Pink (B), 1 ball 100R New York White (C).

Hook

US Size J/10 (6 mm) crochet hook. Adjust hook size if necessary to obtain correct gauge.

Notions

Stitch marker

Fiberfill

Yarn needle

Scissors

Gauge

Gauge is not critical to this project.

Center circle measures 3" (7.5 cm).

Notes

- ♥ This pillow is worked from the center circle out in two panels that are seamed together and stuffed.
- ♥ Small, flat inserts are sewn between each petal.
- ♥ Daisy appliqués are sewn on at the end.
- ♥ Ch 1 does not count as a stitch.

STYLE LIKE STYLES

Flower power is a celebration of color. Change each petal to a bright color for a more psychedelic pillow!

CONTINUED

PILLOW CENTER (MAKE 2)

With A.

Rnd 1: Ch 2, 6 sc in 2nd ch from hook; do not join—6 sc.

Place a marker in last sc made to indicate end of rnd. Move marker up as each rnd is completed.

Rnd 2: 2 sc in each sc around—12 sc.

Rnd 3: [2 sc in next sc, sc in next sc] around—18 sc.

Rnd 4: [2 sc in next sc, sc in next 2 sc] around—24 sc.

Rnd 5: [2 sc in next sc, sc in next 3 sc] around—30 sc.

Fasten off, weave in ends.

PILLOW PETAL

With B.

Working on one Pillow Center at a time.

Row 1: Join to any st on Pillow Center, ch 1, sc in next 6 sc, turn—6 sc.

Row 2: Ch 1, sc in next 6 sc, turn.

Row 3: Ch 1, 2 sc in next sc, sc in each sc across to last sc, 2 sc in last sc, turn—8 sc.

Row 4: Ch 1, sc in each sc across, turn.

Rows 5–16: Rep Rows 3 and 4—20 sc after Row 16.

Row 17: Ch 1, sc in each sc across, turn.

Row 18: Ch 1, sc in 1st sc, sc2tog, sc in each sc across to last 3 sc, sc2tog, sc in last sc, turn—18 sc.

Rows 19–25: Rep Row 18—4 sc after Row 25.

Row 26: Ch 1, sc in each sc across—4 sc.

Fasten off, weave in ends.

Rep Rows 1–26 in the next 6 sts of Pillow Center 4 more times for a total of 5 Pillow Petals.

Rep Pillow Petal instructions for the 2nd Pillow Center to complete the 2nd panel.

SEAMING

With B.

With both Pillow Centers together (wrong sides facing), seam pillow by single crocheting through the back loops only of both thicknesses around. Stuff Pillow as work progresses.

Rnd 1: Join to bottom right side of any petal, *work 24 sc evenly across row ends of side edge of petal, 4 sc evenly across top of petal, 24 sc evenly down opposite side edge of petal, sc between this petal and next petal on the Pillow Center; rep from * around all petals—53 sc per petal, 265 sc total.

INSERT (MAKE 5)

With C.

Row 1: Ch 2, 2 sc in 2nd ch from hook turn—2 sc.

Row 2: Ch 1, sc in each sc across, turn.

Row 3: Ch 1, 2 sc in next sc, sc in each sc across, turn—3 sc.

Row 4: Rep Row 2.

Row 5: Ch 1, sc in each sc across to last sc, 2 sc in last sc, turn—4 sc.

Row 6: Rep Row 2.

Rows 7–14: Rep Rows 3–6—8 sc after Row 14.

Row 15 (border): Ch 1, working across row ends, work 14 sc evenly down side, rotate and work 3 sc evenly along bottom edge, rotate and work 14 sc evenly up next side across row ends—31 sc.

Fasten off, leaving a long tail for sewing. Sew insert between Pillow Petals, lining up 15 sts on either side of insert and 1 sc at bottom. Weave in ends.

DAISY (MAKE 7)

With A.

Rnd 1: Ch 2, 5 sc in 2nd ch from hook, join—5 sc.

Fasten off A, change to C.

Rnd 2: (Sl st, ch 2, 2 dc, ch 2, sl st) in next 5 sc, join—5 petals.

Fasten off, leaving a long tail for sewing.

FINISHING

Sew 1 Daisy to the top of each of the 5 Inserts between the Pillow Petals. Sew remaining 2 Daisies to surface of Pillow. Weave in ends.

"It was a pin I had on my guitar strap and we made t-shirts for it, then I saw a lot of t-shirts around. . . . I'd be driving or something and see someone in one, and I started feeling like, 'Oh this is a bit of a thing.'"

— Harry Styles

CHAPTER TWO: HOME SWEET HOME

"Fine Line" Butterfly Tattoo Blanket

Designed by Valérie Prieur-Côté

We picked this song to represent the Butterfly Tattoo Blanket because it has a little bit of everything. Emotional vocals and a huge array of musical instruments build into a final crescendo. It is the same way with Harry's tattoo journey, starting with just a few and then quickly building to upwards of seven new tattoos each year. This blanket features Harry's prominent tattoos, the butterfly and the swallows. It's reported that Styles has somewhere between 50–67 tattoos with 4 cover-ups! The butterfly, which he got in 2013, reportedly represents a transformation for Styles. And the two swallows facing each other are often represented for the departure and return of a voyage. I hope you enjoy crocheting this tattoo "graphghan" as much as we enjoyed making it!

Measurements

55" x 72" (139.5 cm x 183 cm)

Yarn

Worsted weight (#4 Medium)

Shown here: Lion Brand Basic Stitch Anti-Pilling, 185 yds (170 m), 3½ oz (100 g), 100% acrylic: 13 balls 098C Ecru (A), 4 balls 153 Black (B)

Hook

US Size I/9 (5.5 mm) crochet hook. Adjust hook size if necessary to obtain correct gauge.

Notions

Yarn needle

Stitch marker

Scissors

Gauge

14 sc x 16 rows = 4" (10 cm)

Notes

♥ The RS is facing you on even rows, and the WS is facing you on odd rows. Keep the tails on the WS. This blanket is worked from bottom to top.

♥ You can wind the yarn balls into smaller balls to make the color work easier.

♥ For a cleaner color change, while making the last stitch before a color change, you will do as usual except the last yarn over, and pull through will be with the new color.

♥ The charts are to be read starting at the bottom right corner and are read from right to left on even rows and left to right on odd rows.

♥ This project is divided into 3 charts: Ferns, Butterfly, and Birds.

♥ Since this blanket is inspired by Harry Styles's tattoos, once this blanket is done, you can add his smaller tattoos (e.g., the letters A and G or the years) wherever you want on the blanket with black yarn and surface crochet or embroidery techniques.

Special Stitches

Fsc (foundation single crochet): Ch 2, insert hook in 2nd ch from hook and pull up loop, yo and pull through 1 loop (ch made), yo and pull through 2 loops (sc made), *insert hook in ch of previous st and pull up loop, yo and pull through 1 loop (ch made), yo and pull through 2 loops (sc made); rep from * for required number of fsc.

CONTINUED

CHAPTER TWO: HOME SWEET HOME

BLANKET

Row 1 (WS): With A, fsc 186, ch 1, turn.

Rows 2–10: With A, sc in each st across, ch 1, turn.

Rows 11 and 12: With A, sc in next 10 sts; with B, sc in each st to last 10 sts; with A, sc in last 10 sts, ch 1, turn.

Rows 13–37: With A, sc in first 10 sts; with B, sc in next 2 sts; with A, sc in each st to last 12 sts; with B, sc in next 2 sts; with A, sc in last 10 sts, ch 1, turn.

Work Tattoo Patterns

Note: Continue to ch 1 and turn at the end of every row.

Work Fern Charts

Row 1 (RS): Sc in next 93 sts AND change yarn color following Row 1 of Fern Right Half Chart; sc in next 93 sts AND change yarn color following Row 1 of Fern Left Half Chart.

Row 2: Sc in next 93 sts AND change yarn color following next row of Fern Left Half Chart; sc in next 93 sts AND change yarn color following next row of Fern Right Half Chart.

Row 3: Sc in next 93 sts AND change yarn color following next row of Fern Right Half Chart; sc in next 93 sts AND change yarn color following next row of Fern Left Half Chart.

Rows 4–46: Rep Rows 2 and 3 until all 46 rows of Fern charts have been completed.

Next 6 rows: With A, sc in first 10 sts; with B, sc in next 2 sts; with A, sc in each st to last 12 sts; with B, sc in next 2 sts; with A, sc in last 10 sts, ch 1, turn.

STYLE LIKE STYLES

This blanket has the perfect moody fall vibes! Bring it out, light a spice-scented candle, and get ready to cuddle and crochet.

"I like that kind of style of tattoos, like the old sailor kind of tattoos. [The swallows]... symbolize traveling, and we travel a lot!"

— Harry Styles

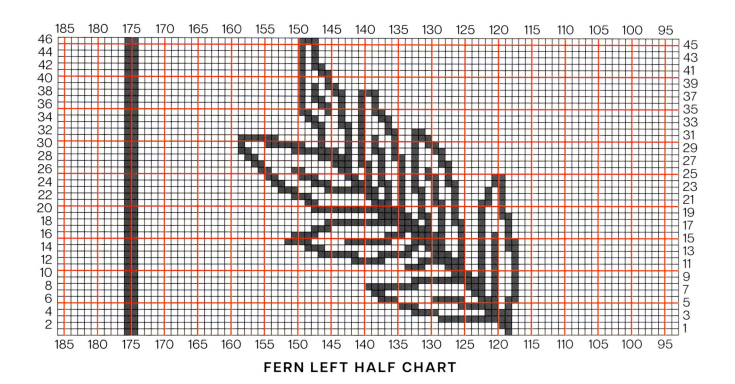

FERN LEFT HALF CHART

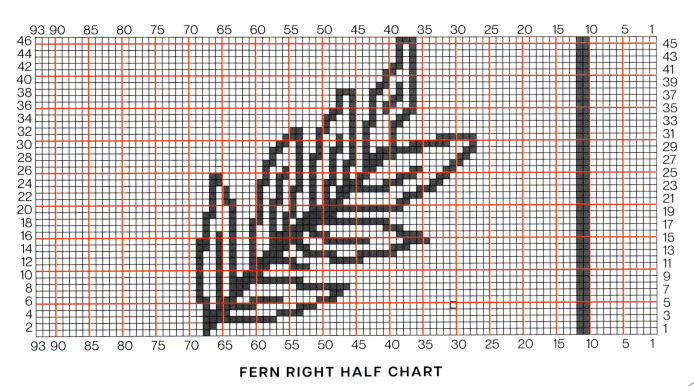

FERN RIGHT HALF CHART

KEY

☐ Ecru (A)
■ Black (B)

CHAPTER TWO: HOME SWEET HOME

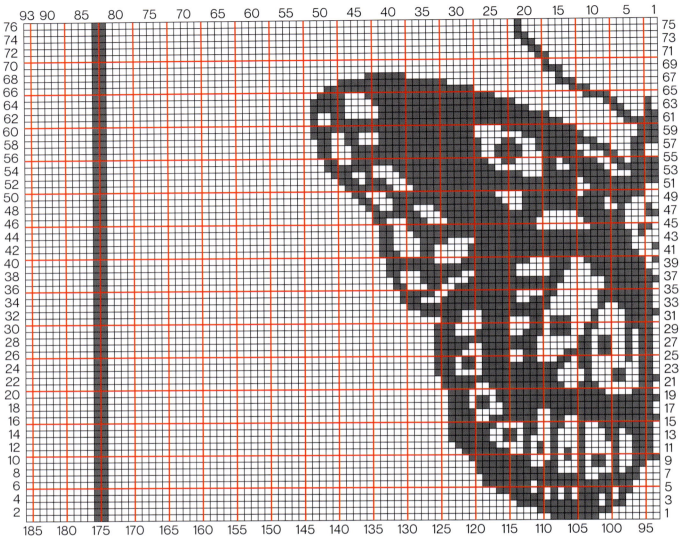

BUTTERFLY LEFT HALF CHART

KEY
☐ Ecru (A)
■ Black (B)

98　UNOFFICIAL HARRY STYLES CROCHET

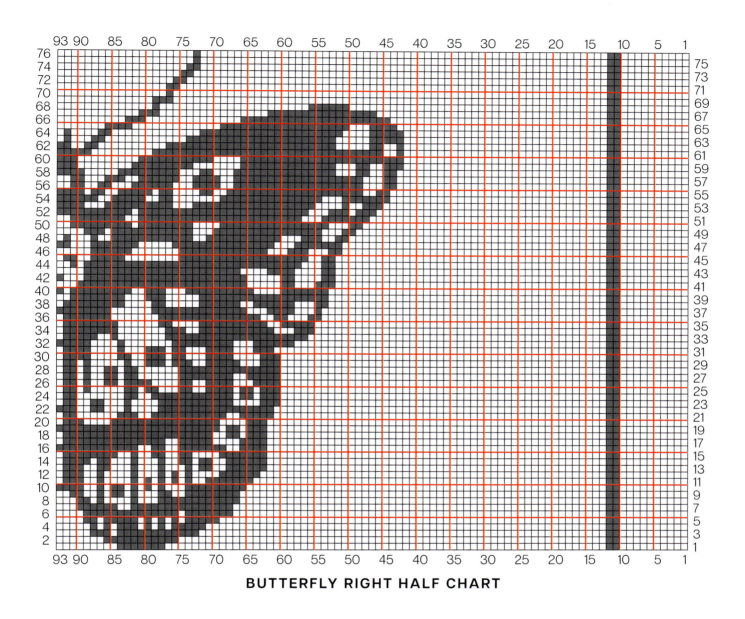

BUTTERFLY RIGHT HALF CHART

Work Butterfly Charts

Row 1 (RS): Sc in next 93 sts AND change yarn color following Row 1 of Butterfly Right Half Chart; sc in next 93 sts AND change yarn color following Row 1 of Butterfly Left Half Chart.

Row 2: Sc in next 93 sts AND change yarn color following next row of Butterfly Left Half Chart; sc in next 93 sts AND change yarn color following next row of Butterfly Right Half Chart.

Row 3: Sc in next 93 sts AND change yarn color following next row of Butterfly Right Half Chart; sc in next 93 sts AND change yarn color following next row of Butterfly Left Half Chart.

Rows 4–76: Rep Rows 2 and 3 until all 76 rows of Butterfly charts have been completed.

Next 14 rows: With A, sc in first 10 sts; with B, sc in next 2 sts; with A, sc in each st to last 12 sts; with B, sc in next 2 sts; with A, sc in last 10 sts, ch 1, turn.

CONTINUED

Work Bird Charts

Row 1 (RS): Sc in next 93 sts AND change yarn color following Row 1 of Bird Right Half Chart; sc in next 93 sts AND change yarn color following Row 1 of Bird Left Half Chart.

Row 2: Sc in next 93 sts AND change yarn color following next row of Bird Left Half Chart; sc in next 93 sts AND change yarn color following next row of Bird Right Half Chart.

Row 3: Sc in next 93 sts AND change yarn color following next row of Bird Right Half Chart; sc in next 93 sts AND change yarn color following next row of Bird Left Half Chart.

Rows 4–35: Rep Rows 2 and 3 until all 35 rows of Bird charts have been completed.

Next 16 rows: With A, sc in first 10 sts; with B, sc in next 2 sts; with A, sc in each st to last 12 sts; with B, sc in next 2 sts; with A, sc in last 10 sts, ch 1, turn.

Next 2 rows: With A, sc in next 10 sts; with B, sc in each st to last 10 sts; with A, sc in last 10 sts, ch 1, turn.

Next 10 rows: With A, sc in each st across, ch 1, turn.

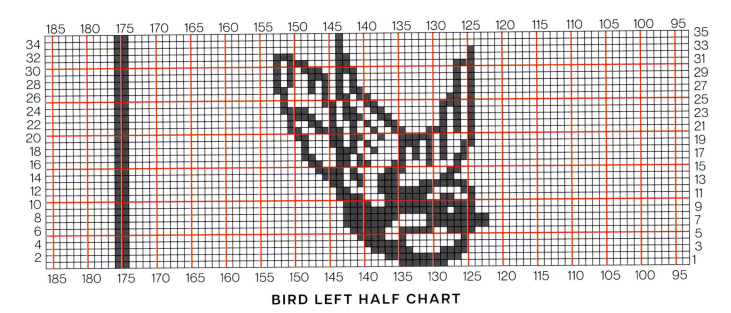

BIRD LEFT HALF CHART

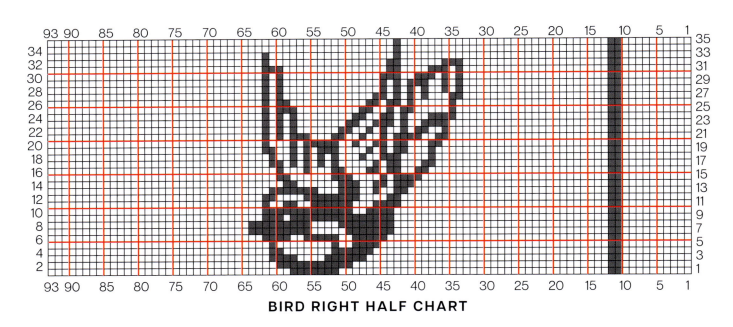

BIRD RIGHT HALF CHART

Border

With RS facing you, join B with a standing sc in the first sc at the top right corner.

Row 1: Sc in each sc across top of blanket, ch 1 at corner; rotate to work across row ends, sc in each row end, ch 1, sc in each sc across bottom of blanket, ch 1 at corner; rotate to work across row ends, sc in each row end, ch 1; join with sl st in first sc.

Rows 2–4: Ch 1, turn. [sc in each sc to next corner ch-1 space, (sc, ch 1, sc) in ch-1 space] 4 times; join with sl st in first sc.

Fasten off.

Weave in ends.

Concert Ready
CHAPTER THREE

Nothing beats getting tickets to your favorite artist's concert and counting the days until you see them perform live! What outfit are you going to wear? What jewelry? Who are you going to go with? Are you going to match, or do your own thing? It's all important, and it's all so fun!

In this chapter, we put together some amazing Harry Styles–inspired concert pieces you can wear out on the town! Starting with the "Satellite" Beanie, a delightful nod to the beanies that young Harry wore when he was starting out, you'll love the beginner-friendly stitches! And in the summer weather, switch to the "Sunflower, Vol. 6" Bucket Hat for those sunny days! The "Canyon Moon" Market Bag features motifs that reference some of the Harry Styles songs we love and is the perfect place to stash all your concert essentials. Take the "Daylight" Dungaree Blanket along to stretch out and enjoy the music at an outdoor concert. Now get out there and show off those amazing crochet pieces; you did such a great job!

"THERE ARE A LOT OF THINGS THAT COME WITH THE LIFE YOU COULD GET LOST IN. BUT YOU HAVE TO LET IT BE WHAT IT IS. I'VE LEARNT NOT TO TAKE EVERYTHING TOO SERIOUSLY."

"Satellite" Beanie

Designed by Lee Sartori

So many of us who crochet spend the majority of our time stitching at home on our own. Although it can be nice to have some quiet time, I think many of us search for a connection in our craft, a community of sorts. Luckily, there are places like social media platforms and groups where we can connect virtually! That longing to belong and share and to be seen and heard is the theme behind "Satellite" as well. Harry Styles sings about the longing in a relationship and about searching for that meaningful connection. It can be difficult to wait to be noticed, but the important thing is that we keep trying our best. Especially for the people who need us the most! The "Satellite" Beanie is inspired by the beanies that young Harry Styles wore when he was beginning his musical journey. The faux knit stitches are beginner friendly but create a texture that is awe-inspiring! You'll want to make one for yourself and all of your crochet-loving friends.

Size

Baby (Toddler, Child, Teen, Adult Small, Adult Medium, Adult Large)

Measurements

To fit head circumference: 12 (16, 19, 20, 21, 22, 23)" [30.5 (40.5, 48.5, 51, 53.5, 56, 58.5) cm]

Yarn

DK Weight (#3 Light)

Shown here: Lion Brand Coboo 232 yds (212 m), 3½ oz (100 g), 51% cotton/49% rayon from bamboo: 1 (1, 1, 1, 1, 1, 2) balls 109T Steel Blue (A), 1 ball each 132 Olive (B), 106I Ice Blue (C), 123Q Tan (D), 157F Yellow (E).

Hook

US Size C/2 (2.5 mm) crochet hook. Adjust hook size if necessary to obtain correct gauge.

Notions

Yarn needle

3 locking stitch markers

Scissors

Gauge

28 sts x 28 rows in stitch pattern = 4" (10 cm)

Notes

- ♥ Hat is worked flat and seamed together at side edge to create a tube. The top is then seamed to close.
- ♥ Yarn color is changed following Stripe Sequence. Fasten off unused colors, and weave in ends as work progresses.
- ♥ Ch 1 does not count as a stitch.
- ♥ Ch 2 does not count as a stitch.

Special Stitches

Exhdc (extended half double crochet): Yo, insert hook into indicated st, yo and draw through 1 loop, yo and draw through 3 loops.

Stripe Sequence

Work *8 rows with A, 2 rows each with B, C, D, E, D, C, and B; rep from * 2 (2, 3, 3, 4, 4, 5) more times for Stripe Sequence.

CONTINUED

CHAPTER THREE: CONCERT READY

BEANIE

With A.

Row 1: Ch 44 (48, 51, 55, 58, 62, 65), exhdc in 3rd ch from hook and in each ch across, turn—42 (46, 49, 53, 56, 60, 63) sts.

Row 2: Ch 1, working in FLO, sl st in each st across, turn.

Row 3: Ch 2, working in BLO, exhdc in each st across, turn.

Row 4: Ch 1, working in FLO, sl st in each st across, turn.

Rows 5–8: Rep Rows 3 and 4.

Rows 9–66 (66, 88, 88, 110, 110, 132): Rep Rows 3 and 4 AND continue to change yarn color following Stripe Sequence (you've already worked the first 8 rows with A).

Joining

With WS facing, sl st last row to Row 1 through both thicknesses. Fasten off, weave in ends.

Seaming

With A.

With a locking stitch marker, lay hat flat on a flat surface. Lock the stitch marker through both thicknesses of center top of hat. Place a second stitch marker on left edge of top. Bring that stitch marker to center by folding edge inward. Place a third stitch marker to right edge of top. Bring that stitch marker to center by folding edge inward. You will now have an X at the top of your hat comprised of 4 corners. Sew each of 4 edges from the center stitch marker toward the outer edge.

Weave in ends.

STYLE LIKE STYLES

Add a pom-pom to the top of this hat for a classic winter look!

"I THINK WE TRY JUST AS HARD AS WE CAN TO JUST BE OURSELVES. I THINK THAT IS IMPORTANT, ESPECIALLY WITH THE WAY THE WORLD IS AT THE MOMENT. THERE ARE SO MANY THINGS TELLING PEOPLE TO BE OTHER THAN THEMSELVES. WE TRY TO BE WHO WE ARE WHILE NOT BEING STUPID."

CHAPTER THREE: CONCERT READY

Love on Tour Bunnies

Designed by Lee Sartori

Skill Level 2

The year was 2020, and the *Love on Tour* concert that had been scheduled to tour around the world was postponed due to the pandemic. Fans were disappointed but understanding and anxiously awaited the tour's return for their chance to see Harry Styles live. After a long wait, the *Love on Tour* show became one of the first full-capacity indoor arena concert tours to occur in the United States since the pandemic, and fans were finally able to celebrate together. Upon arriving at the tour and heading to the merch tables, fans began noticing rabbits everywhere! But what could they mean? An explanation was never officially given, but the popular *Love on Tour* rabbits could be found on bags, sweaters, shirts, and keychains, delighting fans and leaving them with questions and theories. Some possible explanations could be that the bunnies are for Harry's mother, Anne, while others say that the bunnies represent several good omens such as luck, transformation, intuition, and prosperity. Whatever the reason Harry had for the use of these adorable furry friends, they were well-loved! I couldn't resist the cuteness factor of creating some cuddly and squishy amigurumi bunnies for you! Made with ultra-soft Lion Brand Heartland Yarn, these adorable little guys are the perfect way to remember the *Love on Tour* concert as well as make a great gift for a Harry Styles fan!

Measurements

12" x 7" (30.5 cm x 18 cm)

Yarn

Worsted weight (#4 Medium)

Shown here: Lion Brand Heartland, 251 yds (230 m), 5 oz (142 g), 100% acrylic: 2 balls 126U Sequoia (A), 1 ball 098U Acadia (B)

Super Bulky weight (#6 Super Bulky)

Shown here: Lion Brand Hometown Bonus Bundle, 162 yds (148 m), 10 oz (284 g), 100% acrylic: 1 ball each 159K Madison Mustard (C), 148E Portland Wine (D)

Hook

US Size D/3 (3.25 mm) crochet hook. Adjust hook size if necessary to obtain correct gauge.

US Size J/10 (6 mm) crochet hook.

Notions

Stitch marker

Fiberfill

2 pairs of 16mm safety eyes

White embroidery thread

Yarn needle

Scissors

Gauge

Gauge is not critical to this project.

22 sc x 26 rounds = 4" (10 cm)

Notes

♥ Drop unused color behind work for color work section in Head.

♥ All pieces are worked in continuous rounds (spiral).

♥ Ch 1 does not count as a stitch.

Special Stitches

Inv-dec (invisible single crochet decrease): Insert hook in FLO of each of next 2 sts, yo and draw through both sts, yo and draw through 2 loops on hook—1 st decreased.

CONTINUED

CHAPTER THREE: CONCERT READY

HEAD (MAKE 2)

With smaller hook and A.

Rnd 1: Ch 2, 3 sc in 2nd ch from hook; do not join—3 sc.

Place a marker in last sc made to indicate end of rnd. Move marker up as each rnd is completed.

Rnd 2: 2 sc in each st around—6 sc.

Rnd 3: [2 sc in next st, sc in next st] around—9 sc.

Rnd 4: [2 sc in next st, sc in next 2 sts] around—12 sc.

Rnd 5: [2 sc in next st, sc in next st] around—18 sc.

Rnd 6: [2 sc in next st, sc in next 2 sts] around—24 sc.

Rnd 7: [2 sc in next st, sc in next 3 sts] around—30 sc.

Rnd 8: [2 sc in next st, sc in next 4 sts] around—36 sc.

Rnd 9: Sc in each st around.

Begin color work for eyes using A and B.

Rnd 10: Sc in next 12 sts with A, sc in next st with B, sc in next 20 sts with A, sc in next st with B, sc in next 2 sts with A.

Rnd 11: Sc in next 12 sts with A, sc in next 2 sts with B, sc in next 19 sts with A, sc in next 2 sts with B, sc in next st with A.

Rnds 12–14: Sc in next 12 sts with A, sc in next 3 sts with B, sc in next 18 sts with A, sc in next 3 sts with B.

Rnd 15: Sc in next 13 sts with A, sc in next 2 sts with B, sc in next 19 sts with A, sc in next 2 sts with B.

Rnd 16: Sc in next 14 sts with A, sc in next st with B, sc in next 20 sts with A, sc with B.

Fasten off B, continue with A.

Rnd 17: Sc in each st around.

Rnd 18: [2 sc in next st, sc in next 5 sts] around—42 sc.

Rnd 19: Sc in each st around.

Add safety eyes to center of B patches on either side of head.

Stuff Head, continue stuffing as work progresses.

Rnd 20: [Sc in next 5 sts, inv-dec] around—36 sc.

Rnd 21: [Sc in next 4 sts, inv-dec] around—30 sc.

Rnd 22: [Sc in next 3 sts, inv-dec] around—24 sc.

Rnd 23: [Sc in next 2 sts, inv-dec] around—18 sc.

Rnd 24: [Sc in next st, inv-dec] around—12 sc.

Rnd 25: Inv-dec around—6 sc.

Fasten off, leaving a long tail for sewing. Sew remaining 6 sts closed. Weave in end.

UNOFFICIAL HARRY STYLES CROCHET

STYLE LIKE STYLES

For a bit of extra relaxation, add a small pouch of lavender to each of the hearts in the bunnies' paws for a calming scent.

EAR (MAKE 4)

With smaller hook and A.

Rnd 1: Ch 2, 3 sc in 2nd ch from hook; do not join—3 sc.

Place a marker in last sc made to indicate end of rnd. Move marker up as each rnd is completed.

Rnd 2: 2 sc in each st around—6 sc.

Rnd 3: [2 sc in next st, sc in next st] around—9 sc.

Rnd 4: [2 sc in next st, sc in next 2 sts] around—12 sc.

Rnds 5–14: Sc in each st around.

Rnd 15: [2 sc in next st, sc in next 3 sts] around—15 sc.

Rnds 16–19: Sc in each st around.

Rnd 20: [Sc in next 3 sts, inv-dec] around—12 sc.

Rnds 21 and 22: Sc in each st around.

Rnd 23: [Sc in next 2 sts, inv-dec] around—9 sc.

Rnds 24 and 25: Sc in each st around.

Rnd 26: [Sc in next st, inv-dec] around—6 sc.

Fasten off, leaving a long tail for sewing. Do not stuff. Sew Ears to Head starting at center of Rnd 25, and securing along back of Head. Add a slight indent to center of Ears by folding Ears in half longways to create a crease.

BODY (MAKE 2)

With smaller hook and A.

Rnd 1: Ch 2, 6 sc in 2nd ch from hook; do not join—6 sc.

Place a marker in last sc made to indicate end of rnd. Move marker up as each rnd is completed.

Rnd 2: 2 sc in each st around—12 sc.

Rnd 3: [2 sc in next st, sc in next st] around—18 sc.

Rnd 4: [2 sc in next st, sc in next 2 sts] around—24 sc.

Rnd 5: [2 sc in next st, sc in next 3 sts] around—30 sc.

Rnd 6: [2 sc in next st, sc in next 4 sts] around—36 sc.

Rnd 7: Sc in each st around.

Rnd 8: [2 sc in next st, sc in next 5 sts] around—42 sc.

Rnds 9–11: Sc in each st around.

Rnd 12: [2 sc in next st, sc in next 6 sts] around—48 sc.

Rnds 13–15: Sc in each st around.

Rnd 16: [Inv-dec] 3 times, sc in each st around—45 sc.

Rnd 17: Sc in each st around.

Rnds 18–23: Rep Rnds 16 and 17—36 sc at the end of Rnd 23.

Rnd 24: Sc in next 15 sts, [inv-dec] 3 times, sc in next 15 sts—33 sc.

CONTINUED →

CHAPTER THREE: CONCERT READY

111

Rnd 25: Sc in each st around.

Rnd 26: Sc in next 14 sts, [inv-dec] 3 times, sc in next 13 sts—30 sc.

Rnd 27: Sc in each st around.

Rnd 28: Sc in next 12 sts, [inv-dec] 3 times, sc in next 12 sts—27 sc.

Rnd 29: Sc in each st around.

Rnd 30: Sc in next 11 sts, [inv-dec] 3 times, sc in next 10 sts—24 sc.

Rnd 31: Sc in each st around.

Rnd 32: Sc in next 9 sts, [inv-dec] 3 times, sc in next 9 sts—21 sc.

Rnd 33: Sc in each st around.

Rnd 34: Sc in next 8 sts, [inv-dec] 3 times, sc in next 7 sts—18 sc.

Rnd 35: Sc in each st around.

Fasten off, leaving a long tail for sewing. Stuff Body firmly. Sew Head to top of Body at neck between Rnds 13–22 of Head.

LEG (MAKE 4)

With smaller hook and A.

Rnd 1: Ch 2, 6 sc in 2nd ch from hook; do not join—6 sc.

Place a marker in last sc made to indicate end of rnd. Move marker up as each rnd is completed.

Rnd 2: 2 sc in each st around—12 sc.

Rnd 3: [2 sc in next st, sc in next st] around—18 sc.

Rnd 4: [2 sc in next st, sc in next 2 sts] around—24 sc.

Rnds 5–8: Sc in each st around.

Rnd 9: [Sc in next 6 sts, inv-dec] around—21 sc.

Rnds 10 and 11: Sc in each st around.

Rnd 12: [Sc in next 5 sts, inv-dec] around—18 sc.

Rnds 13–14: Sc in each st around.

Rnd 15: [Sc in next 4 sts, inv-dec] around—15 sc.

Rnds 16 and 17: Sc in each st around.

Rnd 18: [Sc in next 3 sts, inv-dec] around—12 sc.

Fasten off, leaving a long tail for sewing. Stuff bottom of Leg, leaving the top of the Leg empty. Sew Legs to bottom center of Body at Rnd 1, and side by side. Sew upper part of Leg along Body to tack them down in a crouching/sitting position. Weave in ends.

TAIL (MAKE 2)

With smaller hook and B.

Rnd 1: Ch 2, 6 sc in 2nd ch from hook; do not join—6 sc.

Place a marker in last sc made to indicate end of rnd. Move marker up as each rnd is completed.

Rnd 2: 2 sc in each st around—12 sc.

Rnd 3: [2 sc in next st, sc in next st] around—18 sc.

Rnds 4–7: Sc in each st around.

Rnd 8: [Sc in next 4 sts, inv-dec] around—15 sc.

Rnd 9: Sc in each st around.

Rnd 10: [Sc in next 3 sts, inv-dec] around—12 sc.

Rnd 11: Sc in each st around.

Rnd 12: [Sc in next 2 sts, inv-dec] around—9 sc.

Rnd 13: Sc in each st around.

Rnd 14: [Sc in next st, inv-dec] around—6 sc.

Fasten off, leaving a long tail for sewing. Stuff tip of Tail lightly leaving rest of Tail unstuffed. Sew Tail to bottom center of Body directly behind Legs.

ARMS (MAKE 4)

With smaller hook and A.

Rnd 1: Ch 2, 6 sc in 2nd ch from hook; do not join—6 sc.

Place a marker in last sc made to indicate end of rnd. Move marker up as each rnd is completed.

Rnd 2: [2 sc in next st, sc in next st] around—9 sc.

Rnds 3–19: Sc in each st around.

Rnd 20: Sc in each st around, sl st in next st, ch 1—9 sc.

Row 21: Sc in next 4 sts through both thicknesses to close top of Arm (do not stuff)—4 sc.

Fasten off, leaving a long tail for sewing. Sew Arm to Body between Rnds 29–32 on either side.

HEART (MAKE 1 WITH C AND 1 WITH D)

With larger hook.

Rnd 1: Ch 2, 3 sc in 2nd ch from hook; do not join—3 sc.

Place a marker in last sc made to indicate end of rnd. Move marker up as each rnd is completed.

Rnd 2: 2 sc in each st around—6 sc.

Rnd 3: [2 sc in next st, sc in next st] around—9 sc.

Rnd 4: [2 sc in next st, sc in next 2 sts] around—12 sc.

Rnd 5: [2 sc in next st, sc in next st] around—18 sc.

Rnd 6: [2 sc in next st, sc in next 2 sts] around—24 sc.

Begin shaping top of Heart.

Rnd 7: Sc in next st and place marker in sc just made, sc in next 11 sts, leaving remaining 12 sts unworked—12 sc.

Rnd 8: Beginning in marked stitch, [sc in next 2 sts, inv-dec] 3 times—9 sc.

Rnd 9: [Sc in next st, inv-dec] around—6 sc.

Fasten off, leaving a long tail for sewing. Sew remaining 6 sts closed. Weave in end.

Stuff Heart and continue stuffing as remaining work progresses.

Rnd 10: Join yarn with sc in 1st unworked st of 12 unworked sts from Rnd 7, and place marker in sc just made, sc in next 11 sts—12 sc.

Rnds 11 and 12: Rep Rnds 8 and 9.

Fasten off, leaving a long tail for sewing. Sew remaining 6 sts closed. Weave in end. Using A, sew a Heart to hands of each Rabbit. Using white embroidery thread, add a small shine mark to right-top side of each Heart.

"BE A LOVER. GIVE LOVE. CHOOSE LOVE. LOVE EVERYONE, ALWAYS."

CHAPTER THREE: CONCERT READY

"Daylight" Dungaree Blanket

Designed by Jennifer Connors

There are a few theories about the meaning behind "Daylight" from Harry Styles's *Harry's House* album. The song references a blue bird that wants to fly away to meet his love, and in the music video, Harry is dressed as a flightless yellow bird. Many fans agree that the song is about the sadness that Harry felt as the *Love on Tour* concert tour was coming to an end. That he wanted to "fly" to his fans and continue performing with them. This theory also fits with the music video depiction of a circus where Harry is performing, again as a yellow bird that cannot fly. It's an interesting theory, and I can see it! For the "Daylight" Dungaree Blanket, we pulled from the circus theme in the music video and the famous sparkly dungarees that Harry wears on the red carpet in the same color palette. This blanket features the "Corner to Corner" crochet technique to achieve the diamonds on Harry's famous pants, a method that is so fun and soothing to work on. Whatever the meaning behind the song is, fans can agree that they love to see Harry Styles continue to tour and perform at his amazing concerts!

Measurements

65" x 90" (165 cm x 228.5 cm)

Blanket is 96 x 130 squares in C2C.

Yarn

Worsted weight (#4 Medium)

Shown here: Lion Brand Vanna's Choice, 170 yds (155 m), 3½ oz (100 g), 100% acrylic: 6 balls 150Z Pale Gray (A), 5 balls each 158I Mustard (B), 172C Kelly (C), 105H Silver Blue (D), 101A Pink (E), 4 balls 146I Dusty Purple (F), 3 balls each 113 Scarlet (G), 109E Colonial (H), 153 Black (I)

Hook

US size K/10 (6.5 mm) crochet hook. Adjust hook size if necessary to obtain correct gauge.

Notions

Yarn needle

Stitch markers

Scissors

Measuring tape

Gauge

6 C2C squares x 6 C2C squares = 4" (10 cm)

The first 6 rows should equal 4" (10 cm)

Notes

♥ Blanket is worked diagonally from corner to corner using the C2C method.

♥ The Blanket is worked by following the instructions and following the chart for color changes.

♥ The chart is read from the bottom right corner to the top left corner. You will be working diagonally and reading the rows from right to left and then left to right. Each square on the graph counts as one block. One block consists of one (sl st, ch 3, 3 dc).

♥ Weave in ends as work progresses.

♥ Decreases begin at the end of Row 97. Mark the end of the row with a stitch marker as a reminder to decrease.

♥ The second set of decreases begin at the beginning of Row 131. Mark the end of the row with a stitch marker as a reminder to decrease.

CONTINUED

BLANKET

Increase Section

Row 1 (RS): With B, ch 6, dc in 4th ch from hook and in next 2 ch—1 square made.

Row 2: With D, ch 6, dc in 4th ch from hook and in next 2 ch; with B, (sl st, ch 3, 3 dc) in ch-3 space at beg of first square, turn—2 squares.

Row 3: With B, ch 6, dc in 4th ch from hook and in next 2 ch, (sl st, ch 3, 3 dc) in next ch-3 space; with D, (sl st, ch 3, 3 dc) in next ch-3 space, turn.

Note: From here on, read color of each square from Chart.

Read all rows of Chart diagonally, reading RS (odd-numbered) rows downward from right to left and WS (even-numbered rows) upward from left to right.

Rows 4–96: Change yarn color following Chart, ch 6, dc in 4th ch from hook and in next 2 ch, (sl st, ch 3, 3 dc) in each ch-3 space across, turn—96 squares in Row 96.

Even Section

Continue to change yarn color following Chart.

Row 97 (RS): Ch 6, dc in 4th ch from hook and in next 2 ch, (sl st, ch 3, 3 dc) in each ch-3 space across to last ch-3 space, sl st in last ch-3 space but do not work any more sts in this space, turn—96 squares.

Row 98: Sl st in first 3 dc, (sl st, ch 3, 3 dc) in each ch-3 space across, turn—96 squares.

Rows 99–130: Rep Rows 97 and 98.

Decrease Section

Continue to change yarn color following Chart.

Row 131 (RS): Sl st in first 3 dc, (sl st, ch 3, 3 dc) in each ch-3 space to last ch-3 space, sl st in last ch-3 space but do not work any more sts in this space—95 squares.

Rows 132–225: Rep Row 131–1 square in Row 225.

Fasten off.

Border

With RS facing, join A at bottom right corner.

Rnd 1: Ch 1, work 3 sc in corner space, sc around the edge, working 5 sc evenly for every two squares, work 3 sc in each corner, join—325 sc per long side, 237 sc per short side, 3 sc in each corner.

Rnds 2 and 3: Ch 1, sc into same sc, 3 sc in next sc (corner), continue to sc around, placing 3 sc into each corner, join.

FINISHING

Fasten off; weave in all ends.

STYLE LIKE STYLES

The circus feel of this blanket definitely calls for some oversized pom-poms in the corners of this blanket! Which colors would you choose?

COLOR DIAGRAM

KEY
- ☐ Pale Gray (A)
- ☐ Mustard (B)
- ☐ Kelly (C)
- ☐ Silver Blue (D)
- ☐ Pink (E)
- ☐ Dusty Purple (F)
- ☐ Scarlet (G)
- ☐ Colonial (H)
- ☐ Black (I)

Scan to access the complete color chart for this project.

"'DAYLIGHT' WAS QUITE AN EARLY SONG ON THE ALBUM. IT WAS... IT'S ONE OF MY FAVORITES AND IT WAS KIND OF A STREAM OF CONSCIOUSNESS WRITING THAT HAPPENED KIND OF LATE. THIS VERY MUCH FELT LIKE, 'OKAY, WE HAVE TO FIND A WAY TO FINISH THIS. NOW.'"

Harry Styles

"Sunflower, Vol. 6" Bucket Hat

Designed by Lee Sartori

One of the best parts of a relationship is doing lots of cute things together. Whether it's running errands or just cleaning the house, it's about the time spent together that counts, and if it ends in slow dancing in the kitchen together, then all the better! "Sunflower, Vol. 6" is about that warm and comforting part of a relationship where everything seems just right. The good outweighs the bad, and life is just . . . nice! Some fans agree that the symbolism of "Sunflower, Vol. 6" is the progression of a new relationship to a seasoned relationship to the end of a relationship, and it begins all over again with someone new. Kind of like a crochet project, don't you think? We get to love it while we work on it, and then when it's finished, we have to move on to something new! The "Sunflower, Vol. 6" Bucket Hat is such a fun project to make and wear. I actually wore this hat out at our local craft store the very day I finished it, and I got so many compliments! One of the staff made it a point to bring her coworker over to show it to her, which really made my day. I hope you get loads of compliments on your finished "Sunflower, Vol. 6" Bucket Hat when you finish yours too!

Measurements
Hat circumference: 20"–22" (51 cm–56 cm)

Yarn
Worsted weight (#4 Medium)

Shown here: Lion Brand 24/7 Cotton, 186 yds (170 m), 100 g (3.5 oz), 100% mercerized cotton: 1 ball 153 Black (A), 1 ball 158R Goldenrod (B), 2 balls 178C Jade (C).

Hook
US Size G/6 (4 mm) crochet hook. Adjust hook size if necessary to obtain correct gauge.

Notions
Yarn needle

Scissors

Gauge
1 square = ½" (14 cm)

Notes
- Hat is worked from the Crown down to the Brim with the Body of the Hat comprised of individual squares that are seamed together.
- Ch 1 does not count as a stitch.
- Ch 2 does not count as a stitch.
- Join to top of 1st stitch with a slip stitch.

Special Stitches

2-dc Cluster (2 double crochet cluster): [Yo, insert hook into indicated st, yo and draw up a loop, yo and draw through 2 loops] twice, yo and draw through remaining 3 loops.

3-dc Cluster (3 double crochet cluster): [Yo, insert hook into indicated st, yo and draw up a loop, yo and draw through 2 loops] 3 times, yo and draw through remaining 4 loops.

Crab St (reverse single crochet): Working in opposite direction of a typical single crochet, insert hook, yo and draw up a loop, yo and draw through 2 loops.

Hdc2tog (half double crochet 2 together): Yo and insert hook in indicated st, yo and draw up a loop, yo and insert hook into next st, yo and draw up loop, yo and draw through all loops on hook.

CONTINUED

CROWN

With A.

Rnd 1 (RS): Ch 2, 6 sc in 2nd ch from hook, join—6 sc.

Rnd 2: Ch 1, 2 sc in each st around, join—12 sc.

Fasten off A, join with B.

Rnd 3: Ch 1, [2 sc in next sc, sc in next sc] around, join—18 sc.

Rnd 4: Ch 2, 3-dc Cluster in first sc, ch 1, [3-dc Cluster, ch 1] in each sc around, join—18 3-dc Clusters, 18 ch-1 spaces.

Fasten off B, join with C.

Rnd 5: Ch 2, 2 2-dc Cluster in each ch-1 space around, join—36 2-dc Clusters.

Rnd 6: Ch 1, [2 sc in next st, sc in next 5 sts] around, join—42 sc.

Rnd 7: Ch 1, [sc in next 3 sc, 2 sc in next sc, sc in next 3 sc] around, join—48 sc.

Rnd 8: Ch 1, [2 sc in next sc, sc in next 7 sc] around, join—54 sc.

Rnd 9: Ch 1, [sc in next 4 sc, 2 sc in next sc, sc in next 4 sc] around, join—60 sc.

Fasten off, weave in ends. Set Crown aside.

SQUARE (MAKE 4)

With A.

Rnds 1–5: Rep Rnds 1–5 of Crown.

Rnd 6: Ch 2, 2-dc Cluster in next 9 sts, [(2-dc Cluster, ch 2, 2-dc Cluster) in next st (corner made), 2-dc Cluster in next 8 sts] 3 times, 2-dc Cluster in same st as beg, dc in beg 2-dc Cluster to join (counts as ch-2 space)—40 2-dc Clusters, 4 ch-2 spaces.

Rnd 7: Ch 3 (counts as tr), 2 dc in same ch-2 space, [hdc in next 2 sts, sc in next 6 sts, hdc in next 2 sts, (2 dc, tr, 2 dc) in next ch-2 space] 3 times, hdc in next 2 sts, sc in next 6 sts, hdc in next 2 sts, 2 dc in beg ch-2 space, join—60 sts.

Fasten off, weave in ends.

JOINING SQUARES TO FORM BODY

With WS facing, sc each Square together with C by stitching from corner tr across to next corner tr through both thicknesses (16 sts per seam) on one side of square. Seam each square in line and seam 1st square to last square to form a ring. Weave in ends. Turn squares RS out.

JOINING CROWN TO BODY

With C.

Rnd 1 (RS): Sl st in 1st dc of any square on top edge, ch 1, [sc in next 14 sts, hdc2tog over next 2 tr on inside seam edge] around, join—60 sts.

Rnd 2: Hold Crown and Body with WS together. Working from RS, sc through both thicknesses of next 60 sts around to join, join—60 sc.

Fasten off, weave in ends.

BRIM

With C, rotate hat to work on bottom edge of Body.

Rnd 1: Rep Rnd 1 of Joining Crown to Body.

Rnd 2: Ch 2, [2 2-dc Cluster in next st, 2-dc Cluster in next 9 sts] around, join—66 2-dc Clusters.

Rnd 3: Ch 2, [2 2-dc Cluster in next st, 2-dc Cluster in next 10 sts] around, join—72 2-dc Clusters.

Rnd 4: Ch 2, [2 2-dc Cluster in next st, 2-dc Cluster in next 11 sts] around, join—78 2-dc Clusters.

Rnd 5: Ch 1, Crab St in each st around, join—78 sts.

Fasten off, weave in ends.

"THERE'S THE WORK AND THE PERSONAL STUFF, AND GOING BETWEEN THE TWO IS MY FAVORITE. . . . IT'S AMAZING TO ME."

STYLE LIKE STYLES
This bucket hat is amazing in cotton, but it would also be great in a jute yarn for a stiffer fabric!

"Canyon Moon" Market Bag

Designed by Lee Sartori

When I first heard the song "Canyon Moon," I immediately fell in love with it. It's so nostalgic for the comfort of home! The lyrics are so bittersweet and filled with longing. For me it makes me think of my time spent at my late grandmother's little wartime house, baking with her in her kitchen and sitting with her on her back porch under her big maple tree. It's a bit sad for me because she's no longer with us, but I am so grateful to have spent that time with her making those memories. She was definitely "home" to me, like the best people in our lives can be. The "Canyon Moon" Market Bag is an ode to some of our favorite symbols from this book. The cherries and the watermelon. The rainbow to remind us about kindness. The ghosts, forever in love. All of them are so fun to crochet and together make a great celebration of all things Harry Styles. I hope you enjoy making them!

Measurements

14" x 3½" (35.5 cm x 34.5 cm), excluding strap

Yarn

DK weight (#3 Light)

Shown here: Lion Brand 24/7 Cotton DK Yarn, 273 yds (250 m), 3½ oz (100 g), 100% cotton: 3 balls 110AR Nightshade (A), 1 ball 157AH Lemon Drop (B)

Worsted weight (#4 Medium)

Shown here: Lion Brand 24/7 Cotton 186 yds (170 m), 3½ oz (100 g), 100% mercerized cotton: 1 ball each of 9 colors:

- ♥ (Watermelon) 142G Rose (C), 100 White (D), 178C Jade (E)
- ♥ (Cherry) 144L Magenta (F), 178C Jade (E)
- ♥ (Two Ghosts) 100 White (D)
- ♥ (Sunflower) 126AA Café Au Lait (F), 158R Goldenrod (G)
- ♥ (Rainbow) 107I Sky (I), 178C Jade (E), 157D Lemon (H), 158R Goldenrod (G), 144L Magenta (F).
- ♥ (Moon) 157D Lemon (H)

Hook

US Size C/2 (2.5 mm) crochet hook. Adjust hook size if necessary to obtain correct gauge.

Notions

Black embroidery thread

Yarn needle

Scissors

Stitch marker

Gauge

Gauge is not critical to this project.

1 granny square = 5" x 5" (12.5 cm x 12.5 cm)

Notes

- ♥ "Canyon Moon" Market Bag is worked in squares that are seamed together.
- ♥ A strap is added after seaming, and appliqués are worked separately and sewn to the front squares.
- ♥ Ch 2 counts as a double crochet stitch.
- ♥ "Dc in top of 1st st to join" acts as a ch-2 space.

Special Stitches

Fsc (foundation single crochet): Ch 2, insert hook in 2nd ch from hook and pull up loop, yo and pull through 1 loop (ch made), yo and pull through 2 loops (sc made), *insert hook in ch of previous st and pull up loop, yo and pull through 1 loop (ch made), yo and pull through 2 loops (sc made); rep from * for required number of fsc.

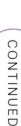

CHAPTER THREE: CONCERT READY

GRANNY SQUARES (MAKE 13)

With A.

Rnd 1: Ch 3, (2 dc, [ch 2, 3 dc] 3 times) in 3rd ch from hook, dc in top of ch-3 to join—12 dc, 4 ch-2 spaces.

Rnd 2: Ch 2, 2 dc in ch-2 space, ch 1, *(3 dc, ch 2, 3 dc) in next ch-2 space, ch 1; rep from * around to beg ch-2 space, 3 dc again in beg ch-2 space, dc in top of 1st st to join—24 dc, 4 ch-2 spaces, 4 ch-1 spaces.

Rnd 3: Ch 2, 2 dc in ch-2 space, ch 1, 3 dc in next ch-1 space, ch 1, *(3 dc, ch 2, 3 dc) in next ch-2 space, ch 1, 3 dc in next ch-1 space, ch 1; rep from * around to beg ch-2 space, 3 dc again in beg ch-2 space, dc in top of 1st st to join—36 dc, 4 ch-2 spaces, 8 ch-1 spaces.

Rnd 4: Ch 2, 2 dc in ch-2 space, ch 1, [3 dc in next ch-1 space, ch 1] twice, *(3 dc, ch 2, 3 dc) in next ch-2 space, ch 1, [3 dc in next ch-1 space, ch 1] twice; rep from * around to beg ch-2 space, 3 dc again in beg ch-2 space, dc in top of 1st st to join—48 dc, 4 ch-2 spaces, 12 ch-1 spaces.

Rnd 5: Ch 2, 2 dc in ch-2 space, ch 1, [3 dc in next ch-1 space, ch 1] 3 times, *(3 dc, ch 2, 3 dc) in next ch-2 space, ch 1, [3 dc in next ch-1 space, ch 1] 3 times; rep from * around to beg ch-2 space, 3 dc again in beg ch-2 space, dc in top of 1st st to join—60 dc. 4 ch-2 spaces, 16 ch-1 spaces.

Rnd 6: Ch 2, 2 dc in ch-2 space, ch 1, [3 dc in next ch-1 space, ch 1] 4 times, *(3 dc, ch 2, 3 dc) in next ch-2 space, ch 1, [3 dc in next ch-1 space, ch 1] 4 times; rep from * around to beg ch-2 space, 3 dc again in beg ch-2 space, dc in top of 1st st to join—72 dc, 4 ch-2 spaces, 20 ch-1 spaces.

Rnd 7: Ch 2, 2 dc in ch-2 space, ch 1, [3 dc in next ch-1 space, ch 1] 5 times, *(3 dc, ch 2, 3 dc) in next ch-2 space, ch 1, [3 dc in next ch-1 space, ch 1] 5 times; rep from * around to beg ch-2 space, 3 dc again in beg ch-2 space, dc in top of 1st st to join—84 dc, 4 ch-2 spaces, 24 ch-1 spaces.

Do not fasten off. Continue to Border.

BORDER

Rnd 1: Ch 1, 2 sc in ch-2 space, sc in each dc and ch-1 space to next ch-2 space, *(2 sc, ch 2, 2 sc) in next ch-2 space, sc in each dc and ch-1 space to next ch-2 space; rep from * around to beg ch-2 space, 2 sc again in beg ch-22 space, dc in top of 1st st to join—124 sc, 4 ch-2 spaces.

Fasten off A, change to B.

Rnd 2: Ch 1, sc in ch-2 space, sc in each sc across to next ch-2 space, *(sc, ch 2, sc) in ch-2 space, sc in each sc across to next ch-2 space; rep from * around to beg ch-2 space, sc again in beg ch-2 space, dc in top of 1st st to join—132 sc, 4 ch-2 spaces.

Fasten off, leaving a long tail for sewing.

SEAMING

Using the layout diagram as a guide, sew 13 squares together using B, and stitch through the back loops only when joining each square. Follow assembly diagram to assemble bag.

WATERMELON APPLIQUÉ (MAKE 3)

With C.

Row 1: Ch 2, 3 sc in 2nd ch from hook, turn—3 sc.

Row 2: Ch 1, 2 sc in each sc across, turn—6 sc.

Row 3: Ch 1, [2 sc in next sc, sc in next sc] across, turn—9 sc.

Row 4: Ch 1, [2 sc in next sc, sc in next 2 sc] across, turn—12 sc.

Row 5: Ch 1, [2 sc in next sc, sc in next 3 sc] across, turn—15 sc.

Row 6: Ch 1, [2 sc in next sc, sc in next 4 sc] across, turn—18 sc.

Fasten off C, change to D.

Row 7: Ch 1, [2 sc in next sc, sc in next 5 sc] across, turn—21 sc.

Fasten off D, change to E.

Row 8: Ch 1, [2 sc in next sc, sc in next 6 sc] across—24 sc.

Fasten off, leaving a long tail for sewing.

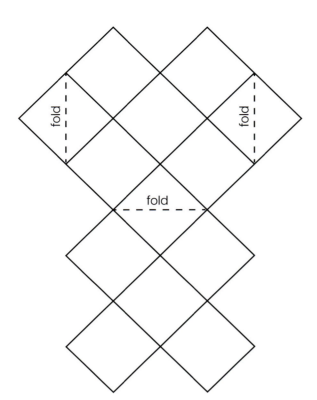

LAYOUT DIAGRAM

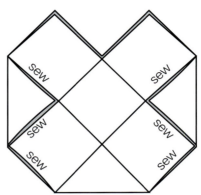

STYLE LIKE STYLES

Sew two watermelon appliqués together and stuff to make an adorable watermelon keychain for this bag or the "Watermelon Sugar" Clutch (see page 50)!

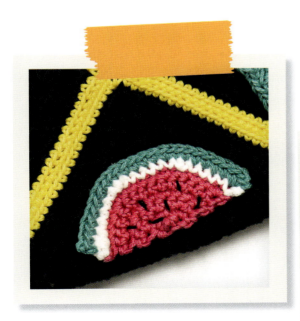

CHAPTER THREE: CONCERT READY

CONTINUED

125

CHERRY APPLIQUÉ

Cherry (Make 2)

With F.

Rnd 1: Ch 2, 6 sc in 2nd ch from hook; work in continuous rnds (spiral)—6 sc.

Rnd 2: 2 sc in each sc around—12 sc.

Rnd 3: [2 sc in next sc, sc in next sc] around, join—18 sc.

Fasten off, leaving a long tail for sewing.

Leaf

With E.

Row 1: Ch 8, 2 sc in 2nd ch from hook, 2 sc in next ch, 2 hdc in next 2 ch, 2 dc in next 2 ch, 7 dc in last ch, rotate to work on underside of ch, 2 dc in next 2 ch, 2 hdc in next 2 ch, 2 sc in next 2 ch, sl st to join—31 sts.

Fasten off, leaving a long tail for sewing.

Stem

With E.

Sl st to 1st Cherry, ch 8, sl st to Leaf, ch 10, sl st to 2nd Cherry.

Fasten off and weave in ends.

TWO GHOSTS APPLIQUÉ (MAKE 2)

With D.

Row 1: Ch 2, 3 sc in 2nd ch from hook, turn—3 sc.

Row 2: Ch 1, 2 sc in each sc across, turn—6 sc.

Row 3: Ch 1, [2 sc in next sc, sc in next sc] across, turn—9 sc.

Row 4: Ch 1, [2 sc in next sc, sc in next 2 sc] across, turn—12 sc.

Row 5: Rotate to work across row ends, ch 1, work 9 sc evenly across row ends, turn—9 sc.

Row 6: Ch 1, sc in each sc across, turn.

Row 7: Ch 1, 2 sc in next sc, sc in each sc across, turn—10 sc.

Row 8: Ch 1, 2 sc in next, sc in each sc across, turn—11 sc.

Row 9: Ch 1, sc in each sc across, turn.

Row 10: Ch 1, 2 sc in next sc, sc in each sc across, turn—12 sc.

Row 11: Ch 1, 2 sc in next sc, sc in each sc across, turn—13 sc.

Row 12: Ch 1, sc in each sc across, turn.

Row 13: *Ch 3, dc in next sc, ch 3, sl st in next sc; rep from * across.

Fasten off, leaving a long tail for sewing. Using A, embroider eyes on Ghosts between Rows 5 and 6.

SUNFLOWER APPLIQUÉ

With F.

Rnd 1: Ch 2, 6 sc in 2nd ch from hook; work in continuous rnds (spiral)—6 sc.

Rnd 2: 2 sc in each sc around—12 sc.

Rnd 3: [2 sc in next sc, sc in next sc] around—18 sc.

Rnd 4: [2 sc in next sc, sc in next 2 sc] around—24 sc.

Rnd 5: [2 sc in next sc, sc in next 3 sc] around—30 sc.

Rnd 6: [2 sc in next sc, sc in next 4 sc] around—36 sc.

Fasten off F, change to G.

Rnd 7: *(sc, hdc) in next st, (dc, tr) in next st, (tr, dc) in next st, (hdc, sc) in next st; rep from * around, join—9 petals.

Fasten off, leaving a long tail for sewing.

RAINBOW APPLIQUÉ

With I.

Row 1: Ch 25, sc in 2nd ch from hook and in each ch across, do not turn, fasten off, leaving a long tail for sewing—24 sc.

Row 2: Join E in 1st st, ch 1, [2 sc in next sc, sc in next 7 sc] across, fasten off—27 sc.

Row 3: Join H in 1st st, ch 1, [sc in next 8 sc, 2 sc in next sc] across, fasten off—30 sc.

Row 4: Join G in 1st st, ch 1, [2 sc in next sc, sc in next 9 sc] across, fasten off—33 sc.

Row 5: Join F in 1st st, ch 1, [sc in next 10 sc, 2 sc in next sc] across, fasten off, leaving a long tail for sewing—36 sc.

Weave in ends from center rows, and use ends from outer rows for sewing.

MOON APPLIQUÉ

With H.

Row 1: Ch 41, sl st in 2nd ch, sl st in next 3 ch, sc in next 4 ch, hdc in next 4 ch, dc in next 4 ch, tr in next 8 ch, dc in next 4 ch, hdc in next 4 ch, sc in next 4 ch, sl st in next 4 ch, turn—40 sts.

Row 2: Ch 1, working in BLO, sl st in next 8 sts; working in both loops, [sc2tog] twice, [hdc2tog] twice, [dc2tog] 4 times, [hdc2tog] twice, [sc2tog] twice; working in BLO, sl st in next 8 sts—28 sts.

Fasten off, leaving a long tail for sewing.

HANDLES

With A.

Rnd 1: Join A with sl st in top of side edge of bag, ch 1, sc in next 33 sc to top peak of right square, fsc 100, skip next 33 sts of same square, skip next 33 sts of next square, starting at peak of 2nd square, sc in next 33 sts, sc in next 33 sts of back square, fsc 100, skip next 33 sts of same square, skip next 33 sts of next back square, sc in last 33 sts of 2nd back square, join—332 sc.

Change to B.

Rnd 2: Ch 1, sc in each sc around, join.

Fasten off and weave in ends.

FINISHING

Using photos as a guide, sew appliques to each of the front-facing squares.

Weave in ends.

CHAPTER THREE: CONCERT READY

"Late Night Talking" Scarf

Designed by Lee Sartori

Having a person in your life that you can tell everything and anything to is one of the most special feelings ever! I am super lucky to have a partner that I get to annoy with all of my thoughts, feelings, jokes, and worries pretty much all day long. Whether it's calling back and forth, texting throughout our workdays, leaving voice memos, or having long chats in the evening, we both rely on each other to get all of it off our minds and can't wait until we do it all over again the next day. We're always thinking about the other person if we are away from each other, wondering what they are doing, how they are feeling, and what they are up to. It's one of those crazy bonds that you have with only the best people. "Late Night Talking" reminds me of just that, the crazy times we get to spend with those loved ones chatting about anything and everything. The "Late Night Talking" Scarf is a nod to a scarf that Harry Styles sports in his music video, where he travels through a portal in his bed in his pajamas. This scarf is worked in a mock knitting stitch using half double crochets and slip stitches together to create a ribbing effect. It's such a cute project, and a great one to make for gift giving!

Measurements

60" long x 5" wide (152.5 cm x 12.5 cm)

Yarn

Worsted weight (#4 Medium)

Shown here: Lion Brand Made With Love The Cottony One, 185 yds (169 m), 3½ oz (100 g), 60% cotton/40% acrylic: 2 balls each 130 Olive Twist (AG), 140X Primrose Hill (B).

Hook

US Size G/6 (4 mm) crochet hook. Adjust hook size if necessary to obtain correct gauge.

Notions

Yarn needle

Scissors

Gauge

Gauge is not critical for this project.

16 hdc x 12 rows = 4" (10 cm) over pattern st

Notes

- ♥ The scarf is worked lengthwise in turned rows, with color changes between each color block of the working row.
- ♥ To change yarn color, draw new color through final yarn over of previous stitch.
- ♥ Cut unused color at each color block change. Scarf is worked in a tube to hide the yarn ends at finishing.
- ♥ Ch 2 does not count as a stitch.

Special Stitches

Exhdc (extended half double crochet): Yo, insert hook into indicate st and pull up a loop, yo and draw through 1 loop, yo and draw through 3 loops.

CONTINUED

SCARF

With A.

Row 1: Ch 242, exhdc in 3rd ch from hook and in next 19 ch, [change to B, exhdc in next 20 ch, change to A, exhdc in next 220 ch] across to last 20 ch, change to B, exhdc in next 20 ch, turn—240 exhdc.

For the remainder of the scarf, alternate between A and B every 20 sts with the corresponding color block.

Row 2: Ch 1, working in FLO, sl st in each st across, turn.

Row 3: Ch 2, working in BLO, exhdc in each st across, turn.

Rows 4–31: Rep Rows 2 and 3.

Row 32 (Joining): Ch 1, with B, sl st through both thicknesses of each st of Rows 1 and 31 to form a tube—240 sts.

Fasten off, weave in ends.

ENDS

Join A with a sl st at beginning of foundation edge.

Row 1: Ch 1, sc evenly through both thicknesses of row ends to close tube.

Rep with B on opposite edge.

Fasten off, weave in ends.

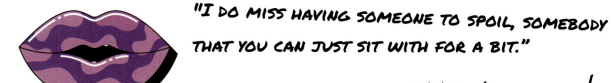

"I DO MISS HAVING SOMEONE TO SPOIL, SOMEBODY THAT YOU CAN JUST SIT WITH FOR A BIT."

UNOFFICIAL HARRY STYLES CROCHET

STYLE LIKE STYLES

Scarves are so versatile! Add some fringe to the bottom edges of your "Late Night Talking" Scarf to give it some flair, or sew the ends together for an infinity scarf look!

CHAPTER THREE: CONCERT READY

Crochet Techniques

BASIC SKILLS

Slip Knot and Chain

All crochet begins with a chain, into which is worked the foundation row for your piece. To make a chain, start with a slip knot. To make a slip knot, make a loop several inches from the end of the yarn, insert the hook through the loop, and catch the tail with the end (1). Draw the yarn through the loop on the hook (2). After the slip knot, start your chain. Wrap the yarn over the hook (yarn over) and catch it with the hook. Draw the yarn through the loop on the hook. You have now made 1 chain. Repeat the process to make a row of chains. When counting chains, do not count the slip knot at the beginning or the loop that is on the hook (3).

Slip Stitch

The slip stitch is a very short stitch, which is mainly used to join 2 pieces of crochet together when working in rounds. To make a slip stitch, insert the hook into the specified stitch, wrap the yarn over the hook (1), and then draw the yarn through the stitch and the loop already on the hook (2).

Single Crochet

Insert the hook into the specified stitch, wrap the yarn over the hook, and draw the yarn through the stitch so there are 2 loops on the hook (1). Wrap the yarn over the hook again and draw the yarn through both loops (2). When working in single crochet, always insert the hook through both top loops of the next stitch, unless the directions specify front loop or back loop only.

Half Double Crochet

Wrap the yarn over the hook, insert the hook into the specified stitch, and wrap the yarn over the hook again (1). Draw the yarn through the stitch so there are 3 loops on the hook. Wrap the yarn over the hook and draw it through all 3 loops at once (2).

Furls Rainbow Streamline Metal Crochet Hook

CROCHET TECHNIQUES

Double Crochet

Wrap the yarn over the hook, insert the hook into the specified stitch, and wrap the yarn over the hook again. Draw the yarn through the stitch so there are 3 loops on the hook (1). Wrap the yarn over the hook again and draw it through 2 of the loops so there are now 2 loops on the hook (2). Wrap the yarn over the hook again and draw it through the last 2 loops (3).

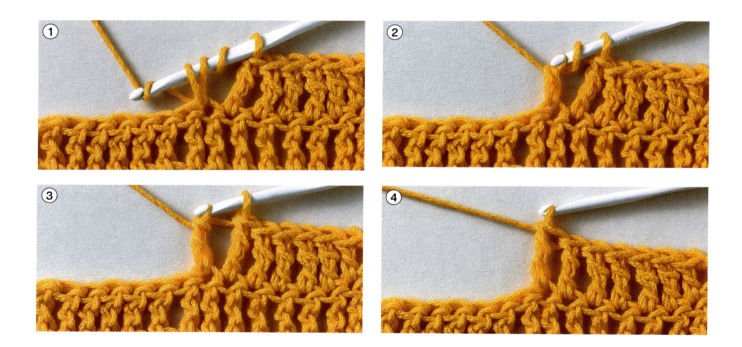

Treble Crochet

Wrap the yarn over the hook twice, insert the hook into the specified stitch, and wrap the yarn over the hook again. Draw the yarn through the stitch so there are 4 loops on the hook. Wrap the yarn over the hook again (1) and draw it through 2 of the loops so there are now 3 loops on the hook (2). Wrap the yarn over the hook again and draw it through 2 of the loops so there are now 2 loops on the hook (3). Wrap the yarn over the hook again and draw it through the last 2 loops (4).

Working Through the Back Loop

This creates a distinct ridge on the side facing you. Insert the hook through the back loop only of each stitch, rather than under both loops of the stitch. Complete the stitch as usual.

INCREASING AND DECREASING

To shape your work, you will often increase or decrease stitches as directed by the pattern. To increase in a row or round, you crochet twice into the same stitch, thereby increasing the stitch count by 1. To increase at the end of a row, you chain extra stitches, then turn and work into those stitches, thereby increasing the stitch count.

To decrease in a row or round, you crochet 2 (or more) stitches together as directed, thereby decreasing the stitch count. The technique varies depending on which crochet stitch you are using.

Single Crochet Two Stitches Together

This decreases the number of stitches in a row or round by 1. Insert the hook into the specified stitch, wrap the yarn over the hook, and draw the yarn through the stitch so there are 2 loops on the hook (1). Insert the hook through the next stitch, wrap the yarn over the hook, and draw the yarn through the stitch so there are 3 loops on the hook (2). Wrap the yarn over the hook again and draw the yarn through all the loops at once.

Double Crochet Two Stitches Together

This decreases the number of stitches in a row or round by 1. Wrap the yarn over the hook, insert the hook into the specified stitch, and wrap the yarn over the hook again. Draw the yarn through the stitch so there are 3 loops on the hook. Wrap the yarn over the hook again and draw it through 2 of the loops so there are now 2 loops on the hook. Wrap the yarn over the hook and pick up a loop in the next stitch, so there are now 4 loops on the hook. Wrap the yarn over the hook and draw through 2 loops. Wrap yarn over and draw through 3 loops to complete the stitch.

FOUNDATION CROCHET

The no-chain foundation is an alternate way to start a crochet project. This method is especially useful if your beginning chain and foundation row tends to be too tight. Using the no-chain method eliminates this problem as you are making your chain and the first row at the same time. Because you don't start with a lengthy chain, this method is also very useful when making a large project, such as an afghan.

Foundation Single Crochet

Chain 2. Insert the hook under the top 2 loops of the 2nd chain, yarn over hook, and pull loop through the chain (2 loops on hook), yarn over, pull through 1 loop (2 loops on hook) (1). Yarn over hook, pull through both loops on hook (one loop left on hook), first stitch completed (2). Insert hook under both strands of the foundation chain of the stitch just made (3). Yarn over, pull loop through chain, yarn over, pull through 1 loop (4). Yarn over, pull through both loops on hook (1 loop on hook), second stitch completed (5). Repeat from * for desired length (6). Turn and work the first row after the foundation (7).

CROCHET TECHNIQUES

SEAMS

There are many ways to join seams in needlework. The ideal seam is flat with no bulk. You can use different kinds of seams in the same garment. Always pin your pieces together before starting to sew.

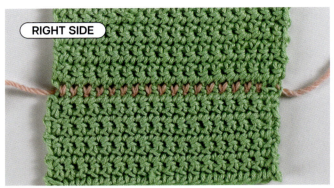

Slip-Stitch Seam

The slip-stitch join is a favorite of many because it joins pieces easily. Your stitches must be worked loosely to avoid puckering seams. Place right sides together, draw up a loop 1 stitch from the edge of seam, insert hook in next stitch, and draw up a loop; continue in this manner until seam is completed.

Whipstitch Seam

The whipstitch seam works best for sewing straight-edged seams. Holding right sides together, insert needle from front to back through inside loops, bring through and around, and repeat.

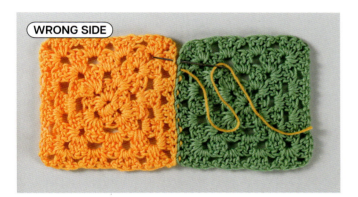 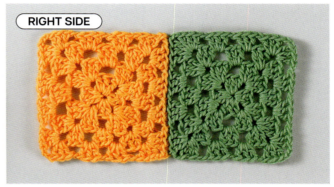

Weave Seam

Hold pieces to be seamed side by side and, working from the wrong side, insert needle from front to back, through 1 loop only, draw through, progress to next stitch, bring needle from back to front (not over), and proceed in this manner until seam is completed. If you draw through top loop only, a decorative ridge will be left on the right side of work. If you draw through bottom loops, the ridge will be inside work.

 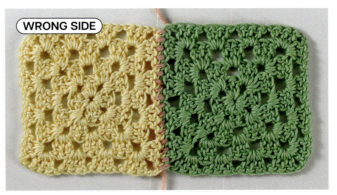

Single Crochet Seam

The single crochet seam creates a decorative ridge; it is especially nice for joining motifs. Holding the pieces, wrong sides together, work single crochet through the whole stitch on both motifs.

CROCHET TECHNIQUES

INSERTING A ZIPPER

When you insert a zipper into a garment seam, you want the garment edges to close over the zipper teeth but still allow the zipper to operate freely. Follow these steps for properly inserting a zipper:

1. Baste the garment edges together with a contrasting thread, using the weave seam method.

2. Center the zipper face-down over the seam on the wrong side of the garment. Pin the zipper in place along both sides of the teeth.

3. Using matching thread, hand stitch the zipper to the garment using a running stitch down the center of each side, and then whipstitch the edges. By catching only the inner layer of the crocheted fabric, the zipper insertion will be nearly invisible from the right side. Turn back the tape ends at the top of the zipper and stitch them in place.

4. Remove the basting stitches from the right side.

ABOUT THE AUTHOR

Lee Sartori is the crochet designer behind CoCo Crochet Lee. Author of several popular crochet books, she can be seen as a guest host on the popular PBS/CreateTV show *Knit and Crochet Now*, and a featured instructor on SkillShare, where she demonstrates fun crochet skills and patterns. Lee's passion is designing modern, wearable garments and adorable amigurumi. Lee lives in Halifax, Canada, with her two children, Noël and Conan, her amazing husband, Sean, her adorable bunny, Neville, and two cats, Ginny and Toast. You can find her work on her blog and on social media, where she posts fun and whimsical takes on crochet.

INDEX

2-dc Cluster (2 double crochet cluster), 119
3-dc Cluster (3 double crochet cluster), 119

A
abbreviations, 14
"Adore You," 45
"Adore You" Strawberry Halter Top, 45–49
albums
    Fine Line (2019), 39
    Harry's House (2022), 69, 79, 115
    Harry Styles (2017), 91
"As It Was," 25
"As It Was" Harry Styles Doll, 25–31

B
Ballmer, Meghan: "Golden" Cardigan, 39–43
Beanie, "Satellite," 105–107
Blanket, "Daylight" Dungaree, 115–117
Blanket, "Fine Line" Butterfly Tattoo, 95–101
Bowie, David, 91
Bucket Hat, "Sunflower, Vol. 6," 119–121
Bunnies, *Love on Tour*, 109–113

C
"Canyon Moon," 123
"Canyon Moon" Market Bag, 123–127
Cardigan, "Golden," 39–43
"Cherry," 55
"Cherry" Earrings, 55–57
Clutch, "Watermelon Sugar," 51–53
Coasters, "Matilda" Tea and Toast, 79–83
Connors, Jennifer: "Daylight" Dungaree Blanket, 115–117
conversion chart, 14
Crab St (reverse single crochet), 119

D
"Daylight," 115
"Daylight" Dungaree Blanket, 115–117
Desjardins, Julie: "Two Ghosts" Slippers, 85–89
diagrams
    "Adore You" Strawberry Halter Top, 47
    "Canyon Moon" Market Bag, 125
    "Daylight" Dungaree Blanket, 117ww
    "Falling" Patchwork Pullover, 64, 67
    "Fine Line" Butterfly Tattoo Blanket, 97, 98, 99, 100
    "Golden" Cardigan, 41, 43
    Harry's House Pillow, 71

"Sign of the Times" Black Lace Shawl, 36, 37
"Sweet Creature" Sheep Vest, 21, 22
"Two Ghosts" Slippers, 89
Doll, "As It Was" Harry Styles, 25–31
double crochet, 134
double crochet two stitches together, 136

E
Earrings, "Cherry," 55–57
Elle, Ashlee: "Adore You" Strawberry Halter Top, 45–49
Exhdc (extended half double crochet), 105, 129

F
"Falling," 61
"Falling" Patchwork Pullover, 61–67
Fine Line (2019), 39
"Fine Line," 95
"Fine Line" Butterfly Tattoo Blanket, 95–101
Fsc (foundation single crochet), 95, 123, 137

G
gauge monitoring, 14–15
"Golden," 39
"Golden" Cardigan, 39–43
Grymes, Krysten: "Sign of the Times" Black Lace Shawl, 33–37

H
half double crochet, 133
Halter Top, "Adore You" Strawberry, 45–49
Harry's House (2022), 69, 79, 115
Harry's House Pillow, 69–71
Harry Styles (2017), 91
Hats, "Sunflower, Vol. 6" Bucket, 119–121
Hdc2tog (half double crochet 2 together), 25, 119
Hdc3tog (half double crochet 3 together), 25
Hooks: #2 (1.5 mm): "Cherry" Earrings, 55–57
Hooks: C/2 (2.5 mm)
    "Canyon Moon" Market Bag, 123–127
    "Matilda" Tea and Toast Coasters, 79–83
    "Music for a Sushi Restaurant" Sushi, 73–77
    "Satellite" Beanie, 105–107
    "Watermelon Sugar" Clutch, 51–53
Hooks: D/3 (3.25 mm)
    "As It Was" Harry Styles Doll, 25–31
    Love on Tour Bunnies, 109–113
Hooks: F/4 (3.75 mm): "Golden" Cardigan, 39–43
Hooks: G/6 (4 mm)
    Harry's House Pillow, 69–71
    "Late Night Talking" Scarf, 129–131

"Sunflower, Vol. 6" Bucket Hat, 119–121

"Sweet Creature" Sheep Vest, 19–23

Hooks: H/8 (5 mm)

  "Adore You" Strawberry Halter Top, 45–49

  Harry's House Pillow, 69–71

  "Sign of the Times" Black Lace Shawl, 33–37

Hooks: I/9 (5.5 mm): "Fine Line" Butterfly Tattoo Blanket, 95–101

Hooks: J/10 (6 mm)

  "Falling" Patchwork Pullover, 61–67

  Love on Tour Bunnies, 109–113

  "Treat People with Kindness" Pillow, 91–93

Hooks: K/10 (6.5 mm): "Daylight" Dungaree Blanket, 115–117

Hooks: L/11 (8 mm): "Two Ghosts" Slippers, 85–89

I

inv-dec (invisible single crochet decrease), 25, 69, 73, 109

L

"Late Night Talking," 129

"Late Night Talking" Scarf, 120–131

Love on Tour (2020), 109, 115

Love on Tour Bunnies, 109–113

M

Market Bag, "Canyon Moon," 123–127

"Matilda," 79

"Matilda" Tea and Toast Coasters, 79–83

"Music for a Sushi Restaurant," 73

"Music for a Sushi Restaurant" Sushi, 73–77

P

Pillow, "Treat People with Kindness," 91–93

Valérie Prieur-Côté: "Fine Line" Butterfly Tattoo Blanket, 95–101

Pullover, "Falling" Patchwork, 61–67

R

reverse single crochet, 119

Rowe, Camille, 55

S

Sartori, Lee

  "As It Was" Harry Styles Doll, 25–31

  "Canyon Moon" Market Bag, 123–127

  "Cherry" Earrings, 55–57

  Harry's House Pillow, 69–71

  "Late Night Talking" Scarf, 129–131

  Love on Tour Bunnies, 109–113

  "Matilda" Tea and Toast Coasters, 79–83

  "Music for a Sushi Restaurant" Sushi, 73–77

  "Satellite" Beanie, 105–107

"Sunflower, Vol. 6" Bucket Hat, 119–121

"Sweet Creature" Sheep Vest, 19–23

"Treat People with Kindness" Pillow, 91–93

"Watermelon Sugar" Clutch, 51–53

"Satellite," 105

"Satellite" Beanie, 105–107

Scarf, "Late Night Talking," 129–131

seams

  "Canyon Moon" Market Bag, 124

  "Golden" Cardigan, 43

  "Satellite" Beanie, 106

  single crochet seam, 139

  slip-stitch seam, 138

  "Treat People with Kindness" Pillow, 92

  "Watermelon Sugar" Clutch, 53

  weave seam, 139

  whipstitch seam, 139

Shawl, "Sign of the Times" Black Lace, 33–37

"Sign of the Times," 33

"Sign of the Times" Black Lace Shawl, 33–37

single crochet, 133

single crochet seam, 139

single crochet two stitches together, 136

Skill Level 1: Basic

  "Cherry" Earrings, 55–57

  "Matilda" Tea and Toast Coasters, 79–83

  "Music for a Sushi Restaurant" Sushi, 73–77

  "Satellite" Beanie, 105–107

  "Watermelon Sugar" Clutch, 51–53

Skill Level 2: Easy

  "As It Was" Harry Styles Doll, 25–31

  Harry's House Pillow, 69–71

  "Late Night Talking" Scarf, 129–131

  "Sunflower, Vol. 6" Bucket Hat, 119–121

  "Two Ghosts" Slippers, 85–89

Skill Level 3: Intermediate

  "Canyon Moon" Market Bag, 123–127

  "Daylight" Dungaree Blanket, 115–117

  "Fine Line" Butterfly Tattoo Blanket, 95–101

  Love on Tour Bunnies, 109–113

  "Treat People with Kindness" Pillow, 91–93

Skill Level 4: Complex

  "Adore You" Strawberry Halter Top, 45–49

  "Falling" Patchwork Pullover, 61–67

  "Golden" Cardigan, 39–43

  "Sign of the Times" Black Lace Shawl, 33–37

  "Sweet Creature" Sheep Vest, 19–23

slip knot and chain, 132

Slippers, "Two Ghosts," 85–89

slip stitch, 132

slip-stitch seam, 138

INDEX

songs
"Adore You," 45
"As It Was," 25
"Canyon Moon," 123
"Cherry," 55
"Daylight," 115
"Falling," 61
"Fine Line," 95
"Golden," 39
"Late Night Talking," 129
"Matilda," 79
"Music for a Sushi Restaurant," 73
"Satellite," 105
"Sign of the Times," 33
"Sunflower, Vol. 6," 119
"Sweet Creature," 19
"Treat People with Kindness" (TPWK), 91
"Two Ghosts," 85
"Watermelon Sugar," 51

stitches
2-dc Cluster (2 double crochet cluster), 119
3-dc Cluster (3 double crochet cluster), 119
Crab St (reverse single crochet), 119
decreasing, 136
double crochet, 134
double crochet two stitches together, 136
Exhdc (extended half double crochet), 105, 129
Fsc (foundation single crochet), 95, 123, 137
half double crochet, 133
Hdc2tog (half double crochet 2 together), 25, 119
Hdc3tog (half double crochet 3 together), 25
increasing, 136
inv-dec (invisible single crochet decrease), 25, 69, 73, 109
single crochet, 133
single crochet two stitches together, 136
slip knot and chain, 132
slip stitch, 132
treble crochet, 134
working through the back loop, 135

"Sunflower, Vol. 6," 119
"Sunflower, Vol. 6" Bucket Hat, 119–121
Sushi, "Music for a Sushi Restaurant," 73–77
"Sweet Creature," 19
"Sweet Creature" Sheep Vest, 19–23

T

"Treat People with Kindness" Pillow, 91–93
"Treat People with Kindness" (TPWK), 91
treble crochet, 134
Twist, Anne, 109

"Two Ghosts," 85
"Two Ghosts" Slippers, 85–89

U

US/UK conversion chart, 14

V

Vest, "Sweet Creature" Sheep, 19–23

W

"Watermelon Sugar," 51
"Watermelon Sugar" Clutch, 51–53
weave seam, 139
Westenberg, Wilma: "Falling" Patchwork Pullover, 61–67
whipstitch seam, 139
working through the back loop, 135

Y

Yarn: #3 Light
"Canyon Moon" Market Bag, 123–127
"Golden" Cardigan, 39–43
"Satellite" Beanie, 105–107
"Sign of the Times" Black Lace Shawl, 33–37
"Watermelon Sugar" Clutch, 51–53
Yarn: #4 Medium
"Adore You" Strawberry Halter Top, 45–49
"As It Was" Harry Styles Doll, 25–31
"Canyon Moon" Market Bag, 123–127
"Daylight" Dungaree Blanket, 115–117
"Falling" Patchwork Pullover, 61–67
"Fine Line" Butterfly Tattoo Blanket, 95–101
Harry's House Pillow, 69–71
"Late Night Talking" Scarf, 129–131
Love on Tour Bunnies, 109–113
"Matilda" Tea and Toast Coasters, 79–83
"Music for a Sushi Restaurant" Sushi, 73–77
"Sunflower, Vol. 6" Bucket Hat, 119–121
"Sweet Creature" Sheep Vest, 19–23
Yarn: #5 Chunky: "Two Ghosts" Slippers, 85–89
Yarn: #6 Super Bulky
Love on Tour Bunnies, 109–113
"Treat People with Kindness" Pillow, 91–93

Z

zippers, 140